BOY BYE!

I DO, I DID, I'M **DONE**!

BOY BYE!

I DO, I DID, I'M **DONE**!

Copyright © 2024 by LaTanya Denise DeFreitas

Chief Editor: Donald Cherry

Writer's Block Press
www.writersblockpress.com

All rights reserved. This book or any portion thereof may not be reproduced or used in any manner whatsoever without the express written permission of the publisher except for the use of brief quotations in a book review.

Printed in the United States of America

First Printing, March 2024

"Until you let go of all the toxic people in your life, you will never be able to grow into your fullest potential. **Let them go so you can grow**."

I DO, I DID, I'M **DONE**!

Table of Contents

The *Not So* Foreword — 9

Journey 1: The Faceless Narcissist — 19

Journey 2: The Shifts — 27

Journey 3: The Last Supper — 39

Journey 4: Piece of a Man — 45

Journey 5: Untitled — 53

Journey 6: Loving the Enemy — 59

Journey 7: Detangled Dreams — 69

Journey 8: Breadcrumbs — 81

Journey 9: The (not so) Ugly Duckling — 91

Journey 10: 50 Shades of a Contract — 95

Journey 11: A Series of Unfortunate Events — 105

Journey 12: Blindsided — 113

I DO, I DID, I'M **DONE**!

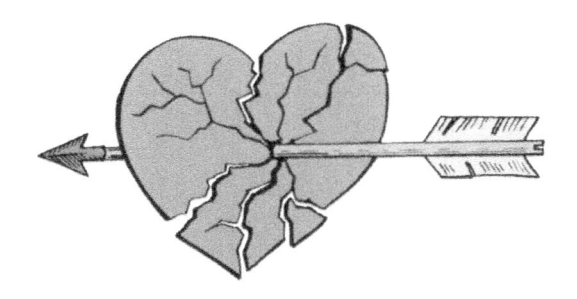

...*Not So* Foreword

Hey Girl!

Can we talk? Isn't love incredible? Feeling loved and being loved is the *most* incredible feeling. Life is a series of ups and downs, especially when it comes to relationships and love. From meeting the one, falling head over heels for them, experiencing happiness... then experiencing the unexpected breakup and the crushing heartache that comes with a roaring "Boy BYE!"

Breakups do not care about your ethnicity, gender, age, sexual orientation, country of origin, or level of popularity. A breakup can be a cruel and merciless experience. No one's life is ruined because of a breakup, is it? But it sure can feel like it.

I was a naive 19-year-old when I first experienced love and heartbreak. In my college dorm room, I cried uncontrollably for what seemed like hours upon hours. I wouldn't eat, couldn't sleep, and was completely absorbed in the here and now.

All the usual emotions like grief, rage, rejection, and loss consumed me. This Mack truck of betrayal slammed into me causing a pain I had never experienced. Tanya Denise was one of the girlfriends who rushed over with a stretcher and bandages to help me get up and get well.

For more than three decades, Tanya and I have worked side by side as classmates, leaders, clients, counselors, business partners, sisters, and friends. We have supported one another through the difficulties of every kind of relationship, including marriage.

In the blink of an eye, we went from being childless college women to moms. We were active in cultural and leadership groups while we were in high school. We went to college together, experienced marriages and divorces, and gained valuable life lessons. As we matured into women, we formed scholarship funds, developed businesses, created nonprofit organizations, and served on administrative boards together. We've done it all: prayed, partied, cried, laughed, succeeded, and failed together. We have even authored books together.

I gladly accepted and sent in my entry when she invited me to participate in the "Boy BYE" collective healing journey. While we experienced many milestones together, we also experienced the journey of healing and growing, hence the reason I did not hesitate to be a part of this project.

Tanya is a woman who fights for women's emancipation and empowerment, in addition to being a business strategist, motivational speaker, and best-selling author on a worldwide scale. Through the ups and downs of relationships and life, we laughed and cried together for more than thirty years. Tanya has been there for me through thick and thin, providing constant wisdom, encouragement, and sisterhood. I've also seen Tanya help other ladies who are going through similar struggles by offering them her unwavering support. You can find that same spark in this book.

Love is patient and love is kind…until it's not. Led by Tanya , Boy BYE will take you on a healing journey through stories of love, passion, heartbreak, and recovery. This anthology will offer wisdom, support, and maybe even tactics to aid in the healing process for anyone who has ever left a toxic relationship or struggled emotionally to do so. It is time: Empowered healing can now commence.

Love and Light,

Tiana L. Burton

Dr. Tiana LaRece Burton

"Just say NO to complicated, dead-end, unhealthy, and toxic relationships."

I DO, I DID, I'M **DONE**!

The following brave women are the contributing authors to this book and the collective healing journey:

Arieka S. Epkins

Cherelle Lenise

Dionne M. Pringle

Dr. Shante Destiny

Dr. Tiana Larece Burton

Effie Clark

Kadana Bryant

Khaila Satee

L.C. Morgan

Nykol Island

Tanya Denise

Xandra Washington

I DO, I DID, I'M **DONE!**

"Being alone may scare you, but being in a bad relationship may damage you."

I DO, I DID, I'M **DONE**!

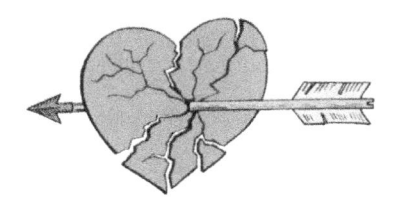

Journey 1

The Faceless Narcissist

We've had a 26-year love affair. He's everything I want, need, and desire in a man. He's charming, and he can be loving. He knows all the right things to say and when to say them.

    I've shared all my past traumas and pains with him. He always listens intensively. Learning them all, play by play, line by line. Hell, he knows most of the war stories better than me. He has learned what makes me happy, what makes me vulnerable, what makes me sad, and my biggest fears of abandonment and rejection that stemmed from my father's unexpected murder. He knows me. It's his best weapon.

    He was my first real relationship. I met him at age 19. I would sneak him into my dorm room in college. I clung to his offers of love and affection, even if they were to keep a roof over his head. A year later, we were pregnant, and that's when everything changed.

He decided to join the military—the Navy, to be exact. It was the closest thing to living in group homes and juvenile detention camps, so he fit right into the structured environment. He gave me hell the entire pregnancy. From claims of not being the father to cheating with multiple women the whole time. I even caught him receiving oral sex from another woman inside the barracks.

There were days I wouldn't eat and was forced to be fed by my homegirls to "feed the baby." I was always a chubby girl. I was at a whopping 390 pounds by my last trimester.

He wasn't there for her birth, but when he came around to be a dad, I allowed him, thinking maybe giving him his own family would make him love me more. When he asked me to marry him, I didn't hesitate to jump into the car and elope in Las Vegas, Nevada.

The night of our wedding, he left me in a strip club while he spent the night with one of the strippers. For the sake of having a husband, I forgave him. I allowed him to reap all the military benefits of having a wife, while I lived life as a 400-pound single mother.

During the next five years, he cheated, verbally abused me, offered tearful apologies, and continued to cheat. I was often told that no one else would want a "fat bitch with a bunch of kids," so every three months, I found myself in the clinic to avoid having a bunch of kids.

Eventually, I graduated college with my master's degree, had gastric bypass to better my health and lose excess weight, and divorced him.

**

I met him on a chatline; he had joined the army and was stationed in Iraq at that time. He knew about the trauma and pain from the previous occurrence, so he always spoke the kindest, sweetest words to me and promised me everything I was missing. He told me I was beautiful. He told me I was smart. He sent roses and he flew out to see me.

He had a wife with whom he was divorcing, and he ensured that I knew I was better than her. Once my divorce was final, I decided to take my baby and move to Atlanta, to be closer to him. Once I arrived and set up, he decided he no longer wanted to be in a relationship.

What did I do now? I was 190 pounds, pretty, educated, and had purchased my own home. But it wasn't enough. He would leave and return; he was always met with an open door and arms.

When he caught a non-curable STD (sexually transmitted disease), I still forgave him and took him back. He was familiar, and I feared the unknown. The last time he left, I begged him to return; he promised he would, but only if I allowed him his "kingly right" to have multiple wives. I contemplated it.

I started working for the city government. We worked side-by-side every day. We would spend 8 hours together, then go home and talk all night. He had a wife at home, but I was his best friend, confidant, and other half. We couldn't tell anyone about our relationship, or we would risk losing our jobs, and his wife might find out.

I had never been "the other woman." For some reason, because his family knew of us and called me "daughter" and "sis," I didn't see it as infidelity. I definitely didn't considered myself a side piece.

For an entire year, he was my entire world. He convinced me that the previous occurrence was the worst thing that could have happened to me and that he was the solution, the divine blessing. God had spoken to him and told him that this was the right time, and I was the one. I believed him.

He provided the perfect bandage to the last experience, and the idea of having multiple wives was blasphemous. His mom would spend the night with me on nights he couldn't because he had to be home with his daughters to protect them from his crazy wife. I remember one night; they had gotten into a physical altercation. He immediately ran to my house, where I tore his shirt, took pictures, and staged the proof of her attacking him. Despite his arrest, I rushed to bail him out. After all, I was his divine blessing and determined to live up to that title.

When I became pregnant with twins, he told me that he was numb. Numb wasn't the response for which I was hoping. I was devastated.

That was our last conversation even though I still saw him daily at work. I still had a relationship with his mother and siblings, yet he treated me like I was a stranger. He never acknowledged my growing belly, although all of our coworkers did.

The night before I gave birth to the twins, he called and asked to be in the room. I agreed. I thought that giving him a family—sons at that—would win him over. The twins were born; he cut the cords and went to work so no one would realize he was absent. I thought that was fair and smart; this was our big secret.

The next night, he returned, looked me in the face, and told me I was a "fucking disappointment." I was in shock. I fell into a depression that would last for an entire year before my family told me it was time to return to

California, sell the house, and move on. I did, full of pain, anger, resentment, rejection, and abandonment for me and my children.

***

He found me again, living in my younger sister's laundry room, sleeping on an air mattress, living out of suitcases with three children, and steadily regaining weight. This time, he moved to California for me. He wanted to be the father of all three kids. He was ready and willing.

I needed to feel this love, especially now. I had hit an all-time low. I had never recovered from the first occurrence, and now we were three blows and three children in.

He was a better man. He wanted to give us everything he hadn't the previous time, and I believed him. This time, he knew how broke and broken I was. He saw how hurt I had been.

I was the provider using child support and public assistance. We argued and argued and argued. To the point where he decided leaving was probably the best option. And he did.

He would return to me for the next 10 years - a different body, a different face. He had different career paths and names but was still the same person. He proposed several times and even married me a few more times. We even had another child together. We traveled together, lived together, laughed, and partied sometimes together, but he was him. He caused the same pain. Each time, the bandages were ripped from the last blow, only to add to the scar and provide more pain. Eventually, you become numb and find comfort in the blows. At least they provide attention and some level of physical interaction. Life continued, but as life continued, so did my sense of self. As I grew my family, I realized the impact he had on me and my most prized possession, my children. I began to educate myself, even going back to school to work on a doctorate. I started women's empowerment businesses and found healing in sharing my experience and gaining strength from other women who had gone through similar journeys. I built a support system, learned not to be ashamed of what I tolerated, and hid under the rug to have him. I found strength in my process of healing from a relationship with him. It's not uncomplicated or over, but it's happening.

Healing is linear and takes many twists, turns, loops, and back peddles. By setting clear boundaries and establishing non-negotiables, I have gained the ability to recognize the signs of gaslighting and prioritize my well-being.

He is a master manipulator. I understand that he will always seek me out due to the love and healing I offer. He will reappear with a different face, attraction, and healing alignment. Still, as I heal, he no longer feels good to me. I have now taken control of my healing journey and my self-worth. I don't want him. I don't want him around my children or to be part of my new chapters. So, when he appears amid my new journey, as I embrace this newfound freedom and power, I confidently look straight into his eyes, smiling the entire time, and say, "Boy, BYE!"

"Sometimes you need to give up on people, not because you don't care but because they don't."

I DO, I DID, I'M **DONE**!

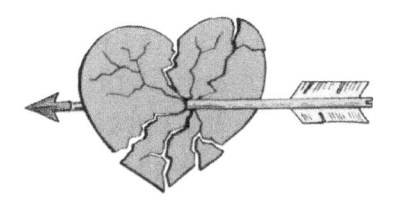

Journey 2

The Shift

I could feel my body fill up with anger and rage. I was trying to wrap my head around being a new mom, completing my first year as a registered nurse, working in the heart of Los Angeles, California, and trying to be the perfect wife. I would never be good enough for him.

I walked into the master bedroom after laying my daughter down for a nap. I walked down the hall and grabbed the screwdriver I had just used to hang up family photos in the hall the day before. With my hand gripping tighter and tighter, I could feel my heartbeat racing, my chest rising and falling heavily, and my breaths becoming deeper and deeper. I stared at the man I once loved with hate in my eyes and betrayal in my heart. I was furious that he could sleep peacefully while causing hell.

I stood over him; I raised the screwdriver, now gripping it with both hands, ready to slam it down on his chest... then my daughter cried. I realized I had too much to lose. But it wasn't until September, when I was arrested, that I realized it was time to say... Boy BYE.

The day that I met Edgar was the day that I should have walked away. He was tall, standing 6'3", almost a foot taller than me. He had smooth, dark, silky skin; he was fit with a smooth, bald, milk-dud head. He had deep brown eyes, a clean-shaved face, a beautiful smile, and charisma. He said all the right things and had the captivating scent of cologne that was so hypnotic.

We met at work. I was 24 years old, working as a certified nurse aide on the night shift, and he was 34 years old, a registered nurse on the unit where I frequently worked. We started conversing about life, and he asked me what I wanted to do besides being a CNA. I told him I was in nursing school but didn't pass my last class, so I was stopped and had to petition, plead my faults, and present a corrective action plan to get back into the program. It had already been a year since I stopped going. I hated jumping through hoops and contemplated starting over from scratch.

We started hanging out, and he helped me with my petition to return to the nursing program. I got back in, and I finished my last year. Within that last year, we started dating and became exclusive. I still lived at home with my parents but would visit Edgar occasionally when I wasn't working or studying.

Things were smooth and easy. He helped me study and had a great sense of humor, so we joked and laughed often. I met his friends, but he never really mentioned his family. He only spoke of them when I asked. Red flag number one.

He told me he was born and raised in Nairobi, Kenya.

He explained that both his parents died in a tragic car accident, and he came to the United States on a student visa several years prior. Red flag number two. None of that bothered me at the time. His story wasn't too far-fetched, and he treated me well until he didn't.

My father never cared for him. He questioned his motives from the time he met him. At my graduation, my dad said he was hiding behind a tree. Now, I cannot confirm or deny that accusation.

When I introduced him to my dad, according to my father, he told him, "This is not a formal introduction. Our formal introduction would be when I shake your hand with this hand and my pistol in the other."

All I can say is that my daddy doesn't play about me because about two weeks later, I had a graduation party at my parents' house, and my dad did just that – with his pistol in hand. But that didn't save me from the wrath of a jealous, selfish, woman-hating, man-child. He wasn't scared of anything or anyone. He was on a mission. I didn't know what that was at the time.

Over the second year of our relationship, he showered me with gifts, trips, and nice dinners. We would go to clubs often and drink, which was when his true colors would show. I wasn't one for clubs, but I went to have a good time with him and loved dancing. Besides, I only had that experience early on because I worked full-time, went to school full-time or both.

At some point within that year, I moved in with him. He had two little girls from a previous relationship. He said the mother wouldn't let him see them. Being the "good girlfriend," I supported helping him gain visitation with his girls. We got engaged then, and three months later, I was pregnant.

Although he had visitation with the girls every other weekend, he wanted more. Being young, naive, and ignorant of his motives, I helped him gain 50/50 custody. Little did I know that it would be more work for me.

On January 3, 2011, Edgar proposed to me. It was the night of his birthday. In March 2011, I found out I was pregnant and in August of 2011, we were married. I was five months pregnant. Two months after our nuptials, what started as verbal abuse became physical abuse. At one time, he knocked me on the floor and put his foot on my stomach. I called my dad to get me and my stuff, and he did. I stayed at my parents' house for about a week and decided I needed to go back and try to work on my marriage.

Shortly after that incident, things were good for a short while. Edgar apologized and wanted to work things out. The next few months were full of love-bombing theatrics. Shortly after, he applied for citizenship and asked if I would sponsor him since we were married. Of course, I said yes and signed all the necessary paperwork to make it happen. At that time, he told me his Visa had expired seven years prior. We were already married, so I didn't see why it would be a problem to help him.

As time went on, we decided to buy a house. Because we were making an equivalent salary, purchased a beautiful six-bedroom 4.5-bathroom home in March 2013. The problem with this was that I was now 2-hours away from all of my family. Red flag number three.

Edgar was always known to be a jealous and extremely controlling person. If I spoke to the opposite sex for too long, if I got too much attention from mutual friends, there was a problem. Since I knew this, I was always reserved around others, dressing modestly, or wearing baggy clothes around men. But this makes no difference when you are dealing with a narcissist.

On September 22, 2013, I got off work from the night shift. I was sitting on the steps at my parents' house, feeding my daughter, when I received a call from Edgar. I answered and said good morning softly because I was tired yet excited to hear from him after a long night at work. I was met with yelling and being called out of my name. When I answered the phone, it was on speaker, so I was fumbling to take it off speaker because my dad was right there, and I didn't want him to hear what Edgar was saying.

You see, all this time, I had been hiding my bruises and protecting my husband as if everything was going well, and it wasn't. I was dishonest with myself, hoping things would improve, but he was a monster.

Once I got the phone off speaker, I quickly handed my daughter off to my dad and walked upstairs. I locked myself in one of the rooms so I could have a private conversation and also try to understand what the fuck he was saying. He was hollering loudly, and deciphering his words over his thick accent was challenging. Immediately embarrassed, I took the 2-hour drive home to resolve our issue. I still carried the obligation of picking up his two daughters on my way home. So, I did that and went to face my fate.

Just a few days prior, Edgar invited his two male friends from the East Coast to visit. He offered to let them stay in our home. I asked why they could not stay in a hotel and said I was uncomfortable with the idea of being in the house with men I didn't know. He brushed off my concerns, and we briefly argued about his friends staying with us. I ultimately gave in.

We went out to a club in San Diego, California, with his two friends, my cousin, and her husband. It was a great night; we celebrated my birthday, but I celebrated a little too much because I left my phone at the club and was without a phone for a few days.

The following night, Edgar had to go to work. I was off work, so I stayed home with his two friends. The two friends stayed in the two rooms we had downstairs. The master bedroom was upstairs. I came down to eat dinner before my husband left for work. I intentionally wore a baggy t-shirt and sweatpants. I knew how his mind operated and didn't want to give him any reason to think I was disrespecting him in front of the company.

I walked him to his car, kissed him and he looked me in the eyes and said, "Behave yourself."

I asked him, "Why would you say that?" "What do you mean by that?"

He just repeated himself and drove off.

I went into the house, straight to my room, and locked the door. I got up the following day. I got the baby ready, and his friends left with me so I could drop them off at LAX (Los Angeles International airport). It only made sense that I dropped them off because I worked at Centinela Hospital Medical Center, in Inglewood, California, and he worked in Corona.

When I arrived home the evening after receiving his embarrassing and disrespectful phone call, we had a big fight - I mean, huge. This delusional man accused me of cheating on him with one of his friends. But it wasn't just the accusation itself that was appalling. The number of details he included with his accusation helped him come up with his definitive conclusion. This man told me not only did I cheat on him, but I used a plastic tampon applicator to insert spermicide into my vagina to have sex with his friend. He said he knew I did it because he found the applicator in the bathroom trash can and took it to the store to ask someone what it was. Psycho right? He didn't listen or want to hear it, no matter what I said. This turned into a shouting match and rolled over to the next day.

On the second day, we still went back and forth. He had so much anger and rage in his eyes. I could tell he hated me. He didn't care for me at all.

After cooking and feeding the kids dinner, I went upstairs with the baby. I stood at the top of the stairs, holding her, tears rolling down my face. I was disgusted, hurt, and ashamed that I had married a man with such hatred towards me. He was not the person I met and fell in love with.

As I stood in my mess, crying, I felt a light pat on my back. It was as if the baby knew what was happening and was trying to console me. As the night went on, I guess seeing me made him angrier. We argued more, and I begged him to leave, but he refused.

At some point, he left, and I locked him out of the house. He had already pushed me around, and I didn't feel safe with him there. I gathered the girls because they were scared and sent them to their rooms. I stayed with them, and suddenly, the lights on the entire house went out. They were crying, and I was trying to determine if the power had gone out or if he had done something.

I gathered the girls into one room upstairs and had the oldest hold the baby while I grabbed the flashlight and checked the house. I was terrified, and on top of all that, I didn't have my cell phone. I heard a loud commotion coming from the downstairs bathroom. He was tearing off the screen, trying to climb through the window. I ran upstairs and locked the four of us in the baby's bedroom.

He made it into the house at some point during the night. We woke up and had a pretty silent day until the evening. That's when all hell broke loose.

Edgar was constantly calling me out of my name, belittling me, and degrading me. Anything he could do to hurt me, he tried. Later that night, after having enough of his games and being physically abused, I decided to fight back. I was only one foot shorter and 65 pounds lighter than he was. But I tried, and I fought back anyway.

I remember standing about five steps up on the staircase and seeing his two daughters standing at the bottom. I was holding the baby on my right hip. This man grabbed me by my neck and threw me down the stairs onto the floor. It was by the grace of God that in a split second, I moved my baby off my hip and in front of me, or I would have fallen on her leg and broken it.

I fought back, and I fought like hell. All I could hear were the screams of the girls and my baby crying.

I remember him being on top of me while I was in a fetal position, trying to protect myself from his blows and yelling, "I can't breathe!"

I remember him holding the back of my neck and shoving my face into the carpet. I remember reaching back, trying to hit him, only to grab my baby's leg, who I could assume was trying to help me.

When I was able to get up, I tried looking for the house phones. We had four wireless phones throughout the house. Every single last one of them was off the hook.

At that moment, he grabbed his two daughters and left. It was just the baby and me, and I called my daddy because that was the only phone number I could remember. As I talked to him, I could hear the phone clicking like it wanted to die. I asked my dad if I should call the police, and he said yes. I'm ashamed to say it, but even at that moment, I was still trying to protect Edgar. I knew that if I called the police, he would run the risk of being deported. But I called them anyway.

While I was on the phone with the officer, Edgar showed up, claiming he wanted his daughters' backpacks. I was too afraid to let him in the house and refused to open the door. Edgar decided to go through the backyard, grab a 5-gallon propane tank, and throw it through the sliding glass door while my daughter and I stood 5 feet away. At that moment, I realized he didn't care about me or my daughter and that's when I decided to say... Boy BYE!.

I DO, I DID, I'M **DONE**!

"Some of us think holding on makes us strong; but sometimes it is letting go."

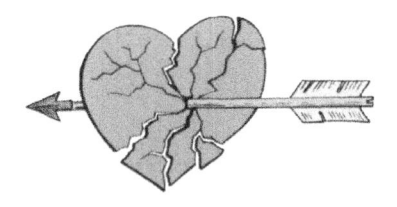

Journey 3

The Last Supper

How dare you leave me sitting in my apartment on Thanksgiving Day, waiting for you to pick me up to meet my mother? You are lucky I have kids because if it were not for them, it would have been some snot-slanging, slow walking, and sad singing behind your dirty casket, but.... I was the dumbass.

He was impressive in his all-black suit, dark shades, and briefcase. He made my knees buckle when he talked with that baritone voice. I hung on to everything he said to me.

We met at work. He was the team supervisor, and I was a contractor just passing through. He would say "whew girl" and with "yo fine ass." It was those three words that made me blush.

We were a part of the same nonprofit organization, which turned me on how he cared for people experiencing homelessness and made decisions to help older people; he was doing so much in the community that I couldn't see that he was just plain fraud. In my eyes, he was perfect because he showed he cared about others. Still, it closed my eyes to the fundamental character flaw.

He was at my apartment day and night. We were together so much.

I never paid attention to the inconsistency until my son said, "Where will that negro be going at 2 a.m.?" I was like, he has to get his son. Lie number 1,235.

He lied so well, or enough to keep me saying *yes, you can come over*. I was willing to do whatever he wanted to do. One full year had passed by before I realized he was married. I couldn't believe he could do me like that, but it was me. I let him do me.

I continued to let him come over after I knew he was married, and he continued to lie to me time and time again. The lies were small, but I believed each one: *she will take my son and move out of state, we are just roommates for the sake of our son, we are getting a divorce soon*. Oh, this was the one that made me say he meant it: "Baby, you complete me. You make me want to be a better person." The best lie he told was "I love you, not her." Boy, BYE!

What the hell does love have to do with it? Having a broken heart may keep you holding the bullets to the gun that kills you. I am keeping it 100%, thinking that my vagina kept me holding on. The mandingo was great. It had me dickmatized. Yeah, I said it. I was mesmerized by that big piece of muscle. The man could look at me and lie and touch me with his tongue, and I was gone.

He did not appreciate me, but I allowed it. I allowed this man to infiltrate my life and my kids' lives and destroy my esteem. It was life after the separation from my ex-husband. I thought we were in it for life, but I was wrong and there I was again. You know why I was wrong again because I didn't love myself.

This ugly, funny-looking bug-eyed sucker dared to come to my apartment after the Thanksgiving weekend for some ass. The nerve of him, no "I am sorry" or anything, just come here with "yo fine ass." Especially with your ugly, skinny, no-car-having ass, and always with an excuse why you have not left the lady you supposedly don't love with the kid that doesn't even look like you at all. I did love myself, and most of all, even when I didn't love myself, God loved me, and I needed to trust that he wouldn't want this for me.

Honestly, it was not even the pain of hurting me that made me let go. When he lied to my mother that made me say enough is enough. My mom is my heart, and even though she knew I would eventually conclude it was him hurting my mom that made me get off the ride. He did not talk to her personally, but he told me to tell her he was coming to meet her. I don't lie to my mother, and I am damned if I let another person make me out to be a liar to her.

My mother said, "Sweetie, only you know when you have had enough." ENOUGH WAS ENOUGH!!!!

I would still see him working in the community doing his thing, but now I see it as redemption, not as a badge of honor. I let go because I am a Queen, and I deserve a King that is mine and mine alone and will treat me as such. I learned a valuable lesson: The Lord will let you make those mistakes you make but will also give you a way out and be right there waiting for you, to pick you up, dust you off, and put you on the right path. If you trust Him, He will return all the blessings you blocked while He was with you if you repent and turn.

One thing I know and two things for sure: GOD loves you and me, and he will never leave or forsake us.

"Bravery is leaving a toxic relationship and knowing that you deserve better."

I DO, I DID, I'M **DONE**!

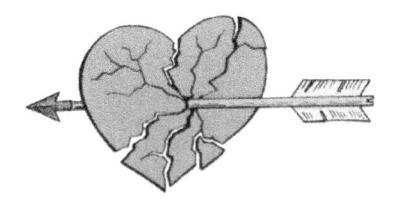

Journey 4

A Piece of a Man

I was sitting on the floor in our bedroom, folding clothes and watching TV. I was excited about my weekend and was getting ready to start in a few hours. My overnight bag was packed in the car, ready to go and enjoy my weekend.

Sitting on the floor, I hear the front door of our apartment slam, my husband bursts into our bedroom, and starts yelling at me. I was sitting on the floor, my heart was racing, and I was thinking, What should I do? What should I say? Should I lie or tell the truth? Will this man hit me if I tell him the truth? What am I going to do? All of these thoughts were in my head.

"You're not going to your sister's house this weekend. You're going to see a nigga!" he yelled.

I looked up at him. I felt fear in my heart. The man I loved so much with all my heart and soul was gone, and now the love was no longer in my heart. So, I told him the truth.

"Yes, I'm going to see another man," and the tears fell from his eyes.

All he could say was, "This is all my fault?"

Let me start from the beginning. Back in 1969, it was just myself and my three children living in the San Fernando Valley of California. I was a very broken woman looking for love. Do you remember when we were younger, and we used to listen to the old school songs by Betty Wright? Shirley Brown and Gladys Knight?

With Shirley Brown the other woman tells her that the man she loves belongs to her. Gladys Knight tells everybody she will get on the midnight train to Georgia because her man is returning to find the world he left behind. She would rather live in his world than without him. And here comes this damn Betty Wright, telling us we are all entitled to make mistakes, and we need to prepare for some heartbreak while we are earning our man and teaching our man no pain, no gain.

So, I was taught to accept whatever a man did. It didn't matter if he cheated, lied, mistreated you, and made you feel like shit. As long as I had a piece of a man, it was better than having no man at all.

So, I met this wonderful man while working at Food 4 Less. He was the most handsome man that I had ever met. He was about 6 feet tall and built very nicely. When I tell you, he was so sexy with a bald head. He was the man of my dreams.

He entered the store, went through my checkout line, and smiled at me. I watched him walk out of the store, looking very good. Well, to my surprise, he came back the next day. I was sitting outside on a break. My break was only 10 minutes. That 10-minute break turned into an hour-long break.

As time went on, we started dating. He did things that a man had never done to me. He treated me well. He would buy me flowers just because, not only one dozen but two dozen, and have them delivered to my job. He would take me out on dates. He loved my children. So, I thought.

Fast forward five years later. We got married, but why did I marry him? To say I had a husband? To make other women feel like I had one up on them or because it was better to have a piece of man than to not have a man at all? Or did I have to feel pain to gain the love I longed for?

Yes, I saw all the signs before I married him. He was the biggest cheater I knew, but because he took care of me and the household, it didn't matter. That's what I was taught.

I just wanted to be loved. I didn't value the woman or the person that I was. He cheated on me with so many women, but the main woman was his daughter's mother. He would do anything for her. If she said jump, he would ask how high, and I would accept it because, again, in my mind, it was better to have a piece of man than not a man at all.

After a while, he started treating my kids bad. He

didn't want to help me support them with the things they needed. I had to start working another job to help pay for my daughter's prom because he did not want to support her. But again, I accepted everything this man had done to me and how he treated my children because I wanted to be loved, and it was better to have a man than no a man.

One day, my husband looked at me and said he didn't want me anymore. When you talk about hurt and pain, he destroyed me on the inside. No matter what he did, I was deeply in love with my husband. I wanted to do everything I could to make my marriage work.

He told me he wanted to run the streets. He told me he wanted to do whatever, but I could still be his wife and say he was my husband. Yes, I cried and stayed with him because it was better to have a piece of man than no man.

I did everything possible to make my marriage work, even if that made me unhappy, as long as he was happy. We even started going to church. He started messing with a lady in church. How humiliating that was.

So, one day, I took to heart what he said to me. Remember, as I mentioned earlier, I had a second job and met a guy there. He was different from any man that I had ever met. I said the same thing about my husband, but this guy was different. He showed me something different in life. He showed me how a man should treat a woman.

I met him in 2008. We are still excellent friends today, and we have a special connection. My husband and I stayed in the same apartment but started living separately. Yes, he wanted to work things out at one point, but I was done because I needed someone to love me and live for me and my children. I'm not saying what I started doing with the other guy was right because it was not, but what I did know was that my marriage was over, and there was no going back.

He knew it was also over when I told him the truth about me going to see another man, not my sister. After telling him the truth, the song "Love Don't Live Here Anymore" by Rose Royce came on the TV. I started singing and crying, tears of happiness for myself. I was finally free from the heartache and pain this man caused me.

That is when I knew it was time to say Boy BYE! I stopped listening to those songs from broken women like I had back in the day. My husband and I divorced in 2013. We were married for 12 years and together for 17 years. If anyone asked him what happened to us, he would always say it was him. I was able to forgive him. We are friends today. We make sure we are doing okay. He has moved on with his life, just as I have moved on with mine.

"Letting go of toxic people in your life is a big step in loving yourself."

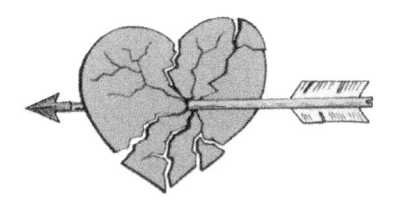

Journey 5

Untitled

What?! I know this nigga didn't! When I first met him, I was in my twenties. I met him while serving in the military. He served, too. He was sitting in the music room, and I walked into the room with my friend. When I saw him, I saw his wrinkled khaki pants, plaid shirt, tilted hat, a confident smirk on his face, and a voice so smooth that it could melt the coldest heart.

    I was immediately attracted to this dude, who didn't seem to have a care in the world. I knew he might be a bad boy. We spent time together that night, and we hung out most nights after that. We had a strong bond and intense love. He was so patient with me and was very kind and understanding. We had a lot in common - maybe a little too much. We were the youngest in our family, came from the same region, minus a few details, and we both went through betrayal and heartbreak. We felt like each other's answer back then.

I built my world around him and had him build inside of me with his seed. We had a family, then got married. The marriage had its good and bad times. However, I walked away because he was still more focused on a single lifestyle and did what single men do.

He did something else, though. He allowed another woman in my home, around our child, and had a full-blown relationship that he tried to deny. I tried to reconcile but saw that he wanted to have his cake and eat it, too, after I gave him a chance. I divorced him when I saw that it wasn't going to work.

Time passed. He started attending church with me consistently. He started being more family oriented. We began to date again. I thought things had changed. He proposed, and I said yes.

It was hard because he started hanging out often, came home at odd times in the morning, and struggled to focus at work. I was trying so badly to keep my family together that I somehow forgot I had to hold myself together. I was haunted by the same eerie feeling that something wasn't right. He traveled to a state without my knowledge during the second marriage, and I had it, so I filed for divorce, again.

We reconciled again and began the process of buying a house. He was away from home to access the papers. He was working and asked that I go into his email to get the paperwork. I had been signing real estate DocuSign and contingencies and setting appointments for inspectors for our new house. It was our half-a-million-dollar home in the most beautiful neighborhood, with a park, grill, and pool. You know the type of home that you need to pay the HOA for.

While searching for documents, what did I see in his email? He has the nerve to be emailing and playing in these women's faces and it had me thinking it was all over. I knew he had acted mean lately but never thought we would be here again.

There I was feeling hurt, sad, and stupid as I read the emails with him. her, and other women, too. The woman he let in our home, our marital bed, the woman I filed papers against, the woman he said I never had to worry about again. The woman I compared myself to and thought I was not enough for him. I would never have long, silky hair down my back, and English is the only language I speak fluently. That doesn't make me less of a woman or less special. The woman he vowed to never go back to.

What hurt was that I gave him multiple chances, and this was many years later—so did they ever break up? I will never know. I was thinking we had passed all of that. I stood with my emotional and mental wounds ripped open again. It is surreal like I was living in a nightmare that would never end.

When I asked him, he said he didn't know what I was talking about. Then, I showed him the evidence. All he could do was admit it. He apologized, but it felt like he was sorry that I found out. Then, he tried to minimize it. Then, I told him the despair I felt and how I felt about leaving this world. He didn't even blink an eye. He was mad at me; can you believe that? That was when I knew I had to leave for good this time.

As a woman, I played myself. The ride-or-die mentality was doing just that, riding on my conscience and killing me on the inside so I could surely die. How can I empower my children when I can't empower myself? I want to live the life I talk about. The relationship would never be the same. I lost all trust in him. It was time for me to heal and elevate.

I knew he could not go with me on the next journey. Yet, it still took a while to get him out of my system. Still, as I started to spend more time praying, journaling, and seeking spiritual enrichment, the desire to enable the mistreatment of my being was no longer attractive.

Submitting to prey was no longer the move. I didn't want the attachment and codependency anymore. I lovingly released him and vowed never to go back. I was lovingly accepted so that I could move forward. I decided to love myself; after all, my daughters were watching. I want them to see that self-love comes first out of all the love in the world!

"Don't stay in an unhealthy relationship because you think it'll get better eventually.
Know your worth and move on."

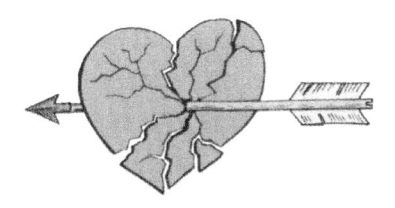

Journey 6

Loving the Enemy

WHY does this always happen to me? HOW do the most intelligent, attractive, career-driven, narcissistic men in Los Angeles, California,. find ME? I mean, maybe it's me! Yeah, go ahead and insert that Kanye shoulder shrug. Perhaps I'm the kind of woman who somehow screams a silent and gentle, "Baby, bring your twisted ass over here" call. Maybe I look safe. Perhaps I resemble a docile doll that can be easily manipulated. The thought is interesting!

Even more enticing is the tremendous mental challenge that's associated with dealing with a narcissist. I've always gotten a high out of great mental stimulation. However, any additives to this type of relationship or situationship can cause things to become disastrous. Let me give you a little taste of my life and how, FINALLY, I could tell this toxic boy BYE!

Growing up, I never experienced the "boy crazy" stage. I was more focused on art, doing hair, and making money. I was a teenage girl who noticed the boys but couldn't care less about their presence. It was the hoes, the jocks, and the nerds who stood out.

One day, God had me zoom in on one of the "hoes." We were cool, but we had our own set of close friends. We would always speak in passing, but only in real conversation if our friends were together. This was probably because he was a year my senior, so we didn't share any classes. He was handsome, and unfortunately, a well-known menace and hoe around the school. He wasn't the type I would glance at, but I paid attention on this particular day. For some odd reason, as we passed one another headed to class, his smile, and his speaking to me were forever burned in my memory. This would someday mean something. What exactly? I had no clue. Yet, I understood that this encounter was different.

Has God ever put someone on your path or radar, and you question the purpose? God NEVER fails to amaze me! When it comes to what He shows me or makes me pay attention to, I'm just in awe. Sometimes, this information is to be used later in life. Baaaby, I couldn't fathom that this little boy, whom I had no interest in, would somehow become my suitor as an adult.

Good 'ol Facebook has a way of allowing people to hunt you like a starving dog, watch you, and strike when they believe it's the right time. Well, here we were, 20-plus years later, and VIOLA! The guy I knew as a kid was now in my inbox. I don't know how this man found me, but he did.

Our conversation started online, which consisted of a little. It was merely fluff, and he made certain advances to establish his interest. Days and nights of conversation then blossomed into much more. I was fresh out of a relationship and wasn't looking for anything serious, so the new conversational pieces were great to pass the time at work. I found out that we had a lot in common. That caused us to cultivate a bond that led to us hanging out frequently and then, eventually, having sex.

WHAT WAS I THINKING? Honey, PLEASE roll your eyes HARD with me! I'm talking about that serious 1990s, "Oh! You must think you're grown now, huh?" "Who in the hell do you think you're talking to?" Your momma is ready to slap you into the 2000s because you just rolled your eyes HARD.

What a horrible mistake to make! LUST is the gateway drug to LOVE. You can get so caught up in how being held, spending quality time, sharing a kiss, laughing, eating together, and simply feeling one's touch can consume you. Together, we spent countless hours, days, months, and years in a tornado of emotions, sex, and fun.

We created great memories. I was there for him in his most challenging times. BABY PLEASE! I wish I could've told myself, "Don't be fooled! You've lost years of precious time that you will never get back, and it's STILL LUST!" I looked up and realized that I was in a whole situationship. Understand that I was 'wrapped up, tied up, and tangled up' in this man, as the elder church folks would say. Sometimes, the thought of him consumed me. I couldn't wait until my kids were out of school, especially for their summer break! My life began to scream the words that rolled off of Juanita's mouth in Baby Boy: "Momma's gotta have a life, too!" Unfortunately, lust can leave you in the position of being the only person loving another. Soul ties are real and a mutha!

"What a beautiful journey is before me," I thought.

I DO, I DID, I'M **DONE!**

I was now low-key delusional! After spending countless years with this man, I fell in love with him. I was able to see a future with him. After all, he had a great career, was handsome, was ok in bed, and could cook his ass off, like me.

We needed to take the time to discuss the future. I kept him away from my family and friends because of it. See, I have this rule. You don't get to be around my family and friends if we're not serious. If by any chance you even exist beyond my knowledge, my children, and a couple of trusted people in my circle (for safety purposes), and we're not serious, then by God, darling, YOU are a miracle! My father taught me that people tend to get twisted in their minds when they meet their family. One may begin to believe that they're something they're not and that you are in a relationship with or a possession of theirs. That always stuck with me. On the flip side, everybody near him knew me and was constantly around us. I never allowed that to go to my head, though.

How was it that everybody loved me but him? Here I was in complete love with this man's representative. It wasn't until about the third or fourth year that the representative decided I was so in love that I wasn't going anywhere. He was finally able to reveal his true self - a selfish coward. I had no clue what I was in for!

The first year of the narcissist's presence had me stumped! I needed clarification about who I had been with all of this time. I was sharing myself with a twisted and hurt man. My love for him blinded me. How did I not realize that something was wrong? Somewhere inside him, he was destroyed. I had no idea what type of man he was until I wanted to share the good news about an accomplishment of mine. I was so proud of myself! I knew he was coming to pick me up that evening, so I held on to my excitement until we got to his house.

"Baby! Guess what?" I was thrilled to share my milestone accomplishment, all for him to defecate on the moment.

Why would he put me down and speak negatively about something so joyous? Where did this come from? His response was so horrid that I had to ask if he'd had a troubling day at work. Not! It was his authentic self. This was just the beginning of the sorrowful years to come.

Where did my charming sweetheart go? I was now dealing with a lying, mean-spirited, manipulative, selfish, opportunistic, entitled, and unstable man who expected preferential treatment, lacked accountability and empathy, refused to be honest about his true feelings unless he was inebriated, and completely disregarded my feelings and boundaries. You would think that I would run. Well, I didn't.

I poured love into him and ignored who I was now interacting with. My loyalty is most times unwavering. I couldn't understand what had changed. I believed that the great man I once knew was still present somewhere. Yeah, the REPRESENTATIVE.

How could someone not be themselves for years? It was like being excited to purchase your first car, only to discover that you bought a lemon. I was devastated, but I wasn't afraid. My baby was lost somewhere, and I was going to find him. It seemed as if the more I loved and complimented him, the more the representative would play peek-a-boo. That gave me hope. However, I got extremely tired of playing mind games and needed fulfillment. We still messed around now and then, but I was able to completely detach myself emotionally. I wanted more for myself! I decided to choose myself and had a desire to be married again. I had wasted enough time with this bull! So, I left.

Being completely single was a mess. I hated it! I wanted to be in his arms. I wanted him to slap my ass while I cooked and then kiss me. Choosing me was challenging, y'all! He'd always call and beg me to come over or go out, but I'd refuse. It wasn't until my father passed that I realized how selfish he was. This man was a nightmare on Elm Street.

After learning about my father's passing by way of a Facebook post, he contacted me and used my grief to bond and lure me back in. Before I knew it, I was trapped. It took a whole year and a half for me to heal and realize what occurred. He was sitting in my face, acting as if he were there to pick up the pieces when, in reality, he had preyed on me. Here I was again, tangled in his raggedy web. I was angry and disgusted with him and myself! THIS was my Boy BYE! moment!

How much love did God place in your heart? So much so that you become a complete fool for love? Being blind is a choice, whether you believe it or not. God told me many times to leave this man alone. I knew he wasn't good for me, but I loved him. God even sent a random lady to prophesy to me and tell me to "STOP PLAYING DUMB WITH THIS MAN! You're too intelligent!"

I fought my protector (God) behind this man simply because I wanted to provide the love Yahweh instilled in me. Baaaaaby, that's what you call crazy! It was my choice to be done entirely.

Through much prayer and supplication, I was able to

move on. I focused on myself and built a stronger relationship with God and those who truly loved me. All the love that I was trying to give to him, I began to give to myself. I could look in the mirror and see ME again - an intelligent, gifted, beautiful, chosen woman of God deserving and available to receive pure and true love, which God sends.

What occurred next was amazing! The doors that were closed due to my disobedience to God opened. My blessings began to flow in like a river! Telling that Boy BYE! and MEANING IT was my blessing!

"Better off alone than with someone who actually makes me always feel alone."

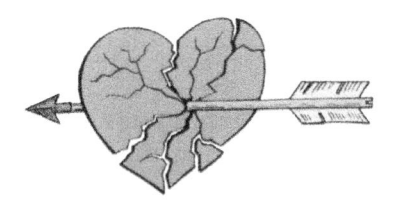

Journey 7

Detangled Dreams

I was not tall, yet not short, with brown skin and a beautiful smile. I was slenderly built yet had a nice shape and I was busty. My eyes were the deepest brown, and my hair was the darkest black. I was a daydreamer who always had her head in the clouds. I always wanted to see the best in others, but somewhere inside, I didn't think others saw my heart.

My beauty was the only thing men wanted to possess, and women tried to destroy it. My thoughts were filled with dreams of being a famous fashion designer. I always wanted to do something for entertainment. I was highly creative and talented.

Yet just as much, and maybe even more than stardom, I wanted the family and love I never had as a child. Not knowing better, the thought of making my life different from my experiences powerfully drove me to perform this task for myself. I could emulate my life like the love stories

I saw in movies and television or the books I read. My mother knew I was destined for a love like that since I had seen many love stories. I thought love was proving myself to men who claimed to have sought that experience of love with me and some who didn't.

Being attracted to him was enough to start a loving relationship. My inner voice was, 'I want him to know that I am a good person.' Even in my friendships, she wanted to be seen and known to have a kind heart. But it didn't seem that people got the message, and they had opinions and thoughts that I didn't understand. I had no idea what I was projecting out to the world, not realizing the hurt and pain of childhood were oozing out of my pores.

I wanted to avoid rejection, but the more I tried, the more it came my way. Those who raised me may not have noticed my kind heart through the walls of abandonment and feeling unloved and unwanted, but they were supposed to be there for me. Some saw my brokenness, and others said I wobbled instead of standing. Some saw me standing and walking confidently and made sure they tore down my hope. Sometimes, I was wandering around like a lost lamb, but surviving in the darkness was what life threw at me. Or they didn't see me because I dimmed my light and played small to be liked, accepted, and understood, and yet I still did not feel understood no matter how hard I tried to paint the picture in their ear.

Clay was so handsome, and when I looked at him, I couldn't help but beam with excitement. The very first day I saw him, I was attracted to him. He was tall and so handsome, and I loved his skin complexion, which was a caramel color, and he had this beautiful curly hair and smile.

His co-worker and friend debated who I was looking at as they walked into the fast-food restaurant to order. As they discussed and then agreed, his friend went into my checkout line, and he went into someone else's checkout line. His friend told him that my smile had left and that it was clear that I was interested in Clay. I didn't have a poker face. I had no idea; I only knew I felt disappointed and thought maybe he wasn't interested. After everyone had ordered, he and I exchanged numbers and started seeing each other often.

At first, everything seemed perfect. We often went to the beach, my favorite place to think and enjoy nature. He drove me everywhere in his car. He'd take me to his place where he lived with his auntie. He introduced me to this local guy who made natural African soaps. On my 19th birthday, he took me to Shakey's on Fairfax and Beverly in the Greater Los Angeles area of California for pizza and conversation. We were both very young. He was 4 to 5 months older than I, and we were in love. We were on that stage, dedicating songs to each other. I loved his style, and he reminded me of Babyface. I would dedicate some of my favorite songs from that artist to him. We shared some of our life stories and some of our life desires.

There came a point where I felt a bit scared of him, and I didn't know why. There were not enough signs, but I kept overlooking minor signs and some I saw. I kept quiet about them and put up with them.

One day, we were over at his aunt's house, and she was there. I joked about something he said and said that was stupid.

He went crazy saying, "Don't call me stupid."

I said I didn't call him stupid, but the thing he said

was. He walked up close to me with a hot iron and held it close to my face like he was going to burn my face. He was threatening me, and worse he was daring me to repeat it. I stopped trying to explain myself and stayed away from him for over a week. But he wouldn't have any of that and would push to see me.

During another visit to his aunt's house, we were watching television and started kissing. His aunt walked in on us, and she didn't like it. I felt embarrassed because I understood and respected older people's opinions. So, I stopped coming to her house. I didn't want her to think of me as the fast girl that was kissing her nephew.

Clay noticed I was no longer trying to spend time with him at his aunt's house. I pulled away from him again and tried to stay away from him. Instead of staying away, Clay drove up to the shelter I was living in, in Hollywood, California, and would be waiting outside in his car at crazy early morning hours waiting for everyone to come out. The girls in the shelter thought it was cute, but I through he was crazy. Yet, I caved in and continued seeing him. He told me he understood that I felt embarrassed but that he was still going to see me. I pushed aside my own thoughts of staying away from him because of his intense desire to stay with me. I started thinking his love was real, he never wanted to leave me, and I saw the intensity as a good man who would be there for me.

It took a while before his aunt and I spoke again. Now living together, Clay and I found ourselves near a payphone checking in on his aunt while she was in the hospital. As she spoke to me over the phone, an air of caution filled her words, warning me to be careful dealing with him. During our conversation over the payphone, Clay was not paying attention to what we were saying and walked away, close to where we were but freeing me to really talk with her.

    Reluctantly, I confided in her about my desire not to live with him. I told her my original plans were to live in the apartment alone but I was pregnant now and so it was for the baby that was coming as well. According to Clay, she had kicked him out and he had nowhere else to go. Her version contradicted his tale. She clarified that he had chosen to leave, claiming that he had another place to go. I disclosed my intention to live independently but he managed to trick me into sharing a home with him.

    A more alarming revelation followed; while she was in the hospital, he falsely reported a break-in at her home. The police were suspecting an inside job. They investigated and found missing items, her jewelry, and her television, according to the evidence. She told me about this and cautioned me, describing him as dangerous. Tragically, she suffered a heart attack and passed away in the hospital.

    Her fear of him was evident and amplified by his lies about his living situation and the theft he orchestrated. Despite the truth being revealed and the warning that was given, I found myself in survival mode, holding onto the information but still staying with him trying to navigate the situation I found myself in.

    Prior to this, I was looking for a roommate in the teen shelters I was in and couldn't find anyone to become roommates with. Everyone else had plans, they found jobs and moved in together and had roommates. I also didn't want to live with anyone, I wanted to live on my own. So, when I found out that I was pregnant, I asked him would he put his name of the lease so that I could have a place for the baby that was coming. He agreed to co-sign so that I could have a place for the baby, yet he was lying to me at the same time.

I did have some fear of Clay prior to finding out he tricked his way into living with me. I was perplexed because I was living with a man that I was not feeling safe with nor was married to and that was not what I wanted for myself. We had our first child together and we ended up getting married. As I dug myself into a bigger hole, I felt a force trying to stop me from marrying him, yet I ignored it.

The broken girl inside of me wanted my dream family. So, I stayed with him knowing the lies he told and seeing a dark side to him. He and I weren't the best at solving conflict, either, but I still wanted my family.

I found myself falling into a life that I didn't plan and wasn't sure I really wanted. During the time we lived living together we had our share of arguments and I kept finding out about his path of stealing things. He claimed he was doing it to provide for the family, but we had enough money to get by.

I tried to only look at the good side of things. I magnified the good I saw in him and ignored the obvious, trying to minimize the characteristics and traits that were not healthy. I looked at how he was the only person that was there for me when it seemed everyone else abandoned me, and how he didn't want to let me go and how he must love me. I made the best of my situation; he did have a good side to him that I loved.

Clay supported my dreams to work in the entertainment industry and he supported my dreams to continue my education. Clay would cook more than I did, and I loved it. I encouraged him to pursue his dreams and education but being in school wasn't his desire. I spoke with him about stopping what he was doing, and he promised that he did.

Yet, he was stealing and doing jobs with a neighbor that he became friendly with. The worst part was he was involved with street men and acting very street because the streets raised him while he was originally from the Bronx in New York. You couldn't look at his outer appearance and tell. He didn't look like he belonged to the street life. Yet it seemed that was what he was gravitating to and maybe he was only looking for his tribe. Like me, he said that he had family but didn't feel the love and support. With his mother gone most of the time traveling to work, he was looked after by his grandmother mostly. But in the neighborhood, the street boys were who he dealt with.

Another lie that he conjured up was that he was fired from his job because his boss didn't feel like he was presentable to work, that his clothes were too wrinkled. I thought that was not a good enough reason to fire someone. He didn't expect me to go to his job to stand up for him.

The shock hit me like a bolt of lightning when I discovered that he had been stealing from his job. I caught the bus from Hollywood to Santa Monica, California, in desperation to defend him. I went to his workplace, pleading with his manager to reconsider, emphasizing his family responsibilities. I spoke with the manager and said that I would make sure that he was presentable for work and that his clothes would be perfectly ironed.

To my disbelief, management disclosed that they opted for termination instead of involving the police, considering that he had a family. He was terminated for stealing.

I was astonished, I exclaimed, "Clay?! Are you sure he was stealing from work!?"

To validate their claim, the manager led me to the office and revealed surveillance footage. The screen displayed Clay, in collaboration with the troublemaking neighbor, covertly moving car parts and other items from the store into the car's trunk. The manager undoubtedly realized that I had no idea what he'd been doing at work. My eyes widened in disbelief as I saw the theft went beyond hearsay and mere speculation. The gravity of the situation struck me deeply. It wasn't just a minor incident, and now he had dragged a neighbor into this troubling web of deceit. The shocking reveal unraveled a darker and more concerning truth that I had ever imagined, or one that I now had to face.

Eventually I gave him an ultimatum to stop stealing all together. I told him that I would rather have a life of integrity and good character and struggle than to steal, lie and cheat in life to get what he wants. I let him know my feelings and if he were to ever go to jail, how that would affect the family overall and that that was not the life I wanted for our children. I let him know that although I wasn't involved in what he was doing I still felt guilty; it was bothering my conscious and it made me feel like an accomplice.

I realized that love wasn't enough to change someone. No amount of begging would stop someone from doing what they wanted. Some people are drawn to do what they shouldn't, and everyone's moral compass isn't the same. For me, enough was enough!

Unknown to me, my father set up my husband after I spoke to my mother about me giving him an ultimatum to leave. My father told him about stealing some hubcaps from a car. But it came back to me from my father that my husband petitioned him to steal caps. Either way, it didn't matter who lied or told the truth, I didn't believe Clay was going to stop.

Does anyone ever know someone from the depths of their soul? Maybe not. Besides the stealing and lying, there was the time he held me upside down while I had our daughter in my arms. I asked him to hold her and somehow that became an argument. He tried to take her and jerk her out of my arms, but I refused to give her to him while he was angry. So, he grabbed me by the ankles and held me upside down as if I were going to eventually let the baby go. But I held on to her tight with one arm and tried to balance myself with the other in mid-air.

I stopped praying for him to get new jobs and he was no longer getting work in Los Angeles. He wanted to move back to New York and work there, he wanted to me to go with him. I told him that I would and told him to look for a place and get a job, get settled in and that I would follow.

The thought was brief., I had come to grip with the fact that he was going to keep doing what he's always done. I didn't follow behind him. I didn't trust him. The hope that I had for him to do better was deflated. He refused to really change.

I got out of the marriage. I divorced him by sending papers to him while he was in New York. I was tempted to stick with him. I loved him. But love wasn't enough for me to take a chance on someone who would continue to steal and get into legal trouble if he were caught by someone who would press charges. It was scary but I ended the marriage and started a new chapter.

"A bad relationship is like standing on broken glass, if you stay you will keep hurting. If you walk away, you will hurt but eventually you will heal."

I DO, I DID, I'M **DONE!**

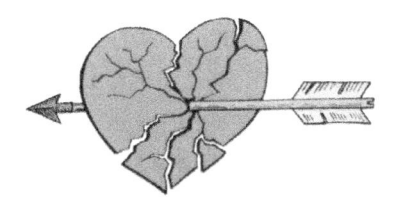

Journey 8

Breadcrumbs

You never know what you invite into your life when you involve yourself with another person. Things may start well, but end badly, leaving you wondering what you missed and when did the person you love change, and why? Most of the time, nothing changed. It is likely that the person you thought you knew was only a disguise for someone they are not. We tend to look past the obvious red flags that ask us to "STOP"! We only yield to keep traveling down that troubled path, wondering where it will lead.

    Wanting love is not bad, but when that want overtakes your sense of reality, it becomes a problem. Ignoring signs that reveal the truth will only lead to heartbreak and sadness. I had a bad habit of trying to see the good in the guys I got involved with. I gave them the benefit of the doubt, while overlooking the fact that they were breadcrumbing me, which is a one-sided situation.

Eventually I realized I was denying myself what I deserved - a piece of the whole puzzle I wanted.

There was one guy that I encountered who was never forthcoming about his intentions but made me *feel* he wanted what I wanted. As I think about it now, I was so foolish because I was verbally revealing what I wanted without realizing I was feeding the narrative of the situation. He followed my lead to satisfy me, keep me quiet for the moment, and get what he wanted.

How could I be so foolish as to believe the feelings were mutual? How could I not see that I was only leading myself down a path that would break me to my core? Am I old enough to know better? I should be because I am way past those teenage years of being naive. Or am I desperate to sell myself short of the love I deserve? Either way, I was cheating myself because you should not have to wonder or try to figure out how someone else feels about you. If love is true, showing and giving love should be easy.

It was September of 2016 when "Brown Eyes" and I crossed paths. No, I was not initially interested. "Brown Eyes" became my little nickname for him because of the color of his eyes, but he never knew this.

I had already been through enough and wanted to clear my head to gain focus on myself so I could get myself together. We worked together but in different departments, making it impossible to avoid each other. I kept my mind occupied, at least for the time being, by doing exactly what I was hired to do as a CNA (Certified Nursing Assistant).

Brief encounters were inevitable, but we remained acquaintances until that one day when he sparked a casual conversation that lasted way longer than I expected it to. I was not interested in the least bit. Still, our conversation ended up being more interesting than I thought.

We became friends and discussed our life experiences, discussing things about ourselves, our children, and past relationships that did not work out. At that time, he was in a relationship that was rocky and on the verge of being over, so I loaned him a listening ear for whatever he was going through. I offered encouragement when he needed it, and eventually, we exchanged numbers to talk more. Over time, our conversations became more frequent, and I began to look forward to the talks because they took my mind off my problems. In the last few months, I had ended a relationship that was never going anywhere. That is a story for another time.

"Browne Eyes" and I became closer than I ever imagined, and he eventually broke up with the girlfriend he was dating. As our conversations continued, we became much closer, and my interest in him began to change. Even though I was not interested initially, something drew me to him. I could not resist this feeling for the life of me, and in all honesty, I did not want to resist.

We soon became intimate, and the universe was like fireworks because the connection was just too good to be true. We never established any titles about what we were to each other, but whatever it was, we were locked in with no plans to let go.

We anticipated seeing each other each day, and it was a feeling beyond anything we could explain. Whatever we felt was very mutual; our souls were intertwined as if we were twin flames. Twin flames are intense soul connections thought to be someone's other half, where their souls mirror each other. I truly believed this was our connection because it was so fierce to let go of once we started.

Every day, we longed to see each other, and even on my off days, we would find a way to meet and see each other. We were inseparable and could not contain what we felt. Still, with no title or strings attached, things were bound to become complicated.

Once sex became involved, feelings soon followed, and this was a disaster waiting to happen. There were questions on my part about what we were because my feelings were becoming stronger, and I knew I wanted to become exclusive. There was no resolution to my questions, and I felt empty. Still, I continued with the "situationship," hoping things would eventually improve. A situationship is a romantic relationship without a clear definition or commitment between two people. This type of relationship weighed heavily on me because I wanted more than he was willing to give me then.

I did not want to lose him, so I did not press the issue, but I knew deep within my mind that the issue would arise sooner rather than later. To be with him for now was just enough to quench my thirst. So, I continued to drink, which satisfied me temporarily.

For months, I went back and forth, trying to figure out what I had gotten myself into. I knew I deserved better but being with "Brown Eyes" whenever and however seemed to override my ability to see things. We were both single, so why could we not be together? Nothing was standing in the way of us being able to commit to each other.

My intuition told me that I deserved more than I was getting, but I continued to settle, not wanting to lose whatever I thought we had. Being with "Brown Eyes" was always breathtaking, but I would feel so empty afterward. This feeling would always make me wonder whether this was a good thing. I knew my feelings for him were valid, but I did not know how he truly felt, which sparked my empty feelings. Out of all the past relationships that I had encountered, something about "Brown Eyes" was so different. The connection between us was no doubt undeniably strong. Still, I did not want to continue giving myself to him if he did not truly value me.

I have had my share of meaningless intimate interactions, and I wanted something more that would last longer than a few months of my life. I was becoming increasingly aware that I needed to be strong and make decisions that may hurt but serve my higher purpose. Yes, I was getting part of what I wanted, but I craved more of what I needed to fill me within.

As a soul starving for soul food, I searched for someone all-in and dedicated. The deeper I became involved with "Brown Eyes," the more I could not shake that empty feeling afterward. He was getting what he wanted, and I was confused, trying to hang on to whatever fantasy I thought it could be.

This situationship lasted for a little over two years, and I could not seem to break free no matter how hard I tried. There was a connection between us that would not dissipate, and my feelings for him were becoming deeper than ever before. The more my feelings grew, the more confusion set in, and I did not like feeling this way. I would go out of my way to show him how I felt, hoping he would reciprocate, but this did not happen. I became very torn about what I should do and what I wanted for myself. I made the situation okay because at least I could spend whatever time I could get with him. Even though I was feeling unfulfilled, being with him anytime was good enough for that brief "good" feeling that I received. I had fallen head over heels for a fantasy I had created in my mind, but somehow I hoped it would eventually give me what I wanted and craved.

As I would override my gut feelings, something deep within me was never satisfied. My urges were always getting the best of me, and I wanted the connection more than anything. Even if that empty feeling appeared, I would not let it get in the way of what my body craved over what my soul desired. I had lost myself once again, searching for something I lacked within and deceiving myself by seeking something that would never suffice.

The breadcrumbing continued, and I became tired of not getting what I deserved. Each moment I sold myself short by being with "Brown Eyes" was nipping away more and more at my inner core. If I knew deep inside myself that I should be fed much more, how could I allow someone to feed me so little?

To love someone, you must first love yourself, and I began to realize that I was not loving myself. Why was I accepting so little when I deserved the world? I knew I would have to make a tough decision. The situation was not good for my mind, body, or soul, and I could not expect anyone else to see this if I did not see it for myself.

As I learned, you teach people how to treat you, and I wasn't modeling that behavior myself. The change in this situation had to begin with me, and no matter how bad it would hurt, I would have to stand up for myself. To lose myself in this fantasy world was more of a loss than to lose this intimate connection. I had to value myself enough to walk away from something or someone not beneficial to me or my journey. Whether he understood or not was none of my concern because I chose to love myself over whatever he and I had superficially created.

    As long as I accepted it, it would not end, so I left to avoid being hurt again. What hurt me the most when I decided to walk away was that he never even asked me why. I then understood even more that I had to choose myself, no matter how badly it hurt me. The revelation of this coming to an end was a bittersweet moment for me. Still, it gave me the confidence to keep moving forward and made me understand why I had to say "Boy, BYE"!

"Breaking up with an unhealthy partner gives you space to get to know what you need in a relationship."

I DO, I DID, I'M **DONE!**

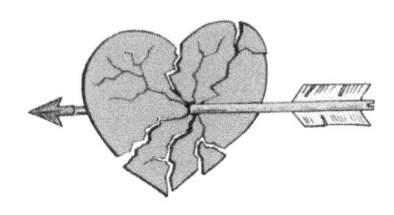

Journey 9

The (not so) Ugly Duckling

Every girl dreams of dating a football or basketball player while attending high school. Well, what happens if that's not your desire? I had a crush on this guy. He was in the Most Popular Boy Crew, known all over campus. We would see each other around campus, and I made sure that he noticed and that I said h. I was good friends with one of the guys on the crew and I asked if he knew if he had a girlfriend.

One day, while walking home from school, he walked the same way I did.

I told myself, *"Here's your chance to make your move or let the opportunity pass you by."*

I had a boldness and a confidence that came over me, and I said to myself, *it's either now or never.* We walked and talked, then exchanged phone numbers. Bingo!

From there, we would talk on the phone for hours. Friends and older cousins told me it was serious when a guy took you home to meet his parents. I had also met a couple of his relatives. So, I was ready.

Finally, the big question was asked: *Would you be my girlfriend?* Of course I said yes, but little to my surprise, he didn't want anyone in our business, which meant no one could know we were together. He would treat me like one of the homegirls. He treated me like a princess whenever we were away from school, which was odd.

Why didn't he want anyone to know? I began to question myself: *Am I not good enough? Am I ugly? What's wrong with me?*

I would ditch school to go to his house. I found out that boys were saying how ugly I was, and he didn't want it to get around campus that he was with me. I was only good enough to be a secret.

I was in an all-girl dance group; we were the baddest girls. We danced and rapped. So, one day, our school had a noon dance, and we had our little biker short outfits. All the boys that talked about me were now following me around. Long story short, we danced at the dance, and all the boys lined up behind us, hawking me. Why? Because I said the same thing. I was a brick house. My shape had them mesmerized.

So, my so-called boyfriend and his crew walked in and wondered what was wrong with these dudes, why they were sitting on the floor, and who and what they were looking at. To his surprise, they were watching me dance. So, he kindly walked up to me, and the guy I was dancing with moved him out of the way and turned around so the boys couldn't watch anymore. So, he wanted people to know we were together because someone else was paying attention to me. Well, Boy BYE, I am a secret chick, remember?!

I DO, I DID, I'M **DONE**!

"You take your power back by letting people go."

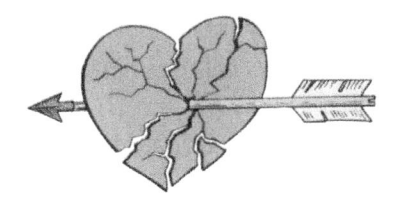

Journey 10

50 Shades of a Contract

DISCLAIMER: The events described within this chapter are to educate, provide support, and release transparency. The details described within this chapter are not fabricated, exaggerated, or sensationalized. I forgive myself and the other party described. This story is not only a lesson but also a guide for other women who find themselves in a similar situation. God has more for you.

The freedom to breathe came over me,
Like that of a tidal wave washing away the heavy current at sea,
The touch of his fingers that ran through my soft hair
Filled my body with dread.
The sweet temptations that once
had me wanting more
It raised my blood pressure, and I couldn't wait to watch his body walk out of my door.

He kissed me softly but stared at me wildly,
He pushed me and pulled me away,
Just to come back and beg me to stay.
Never mind that he knew the Bible
Or that he was black.
It was just business,
Which is why this story is called
50 Shades of a Contract

I was a work-at-home employee of a medical insurance company for almost four years in November of 2018. I was a well-committed employee who was on time, dependable, had a good relationship with my peers, and had dreams of becoming a prolific writer of true crime, thrillers, and memoirs. At this time in my life, I was looking for meaning. I had suffered some pretty horrific events, and I was looking for my place in the world.

    I was sexually molested by an older family member from the age of seven until eleven years old. I was gang-raped at the age of 14 by two boys I hooked up with in high school. Due to the trauma, I suffered in my younger and teenage years, I was an emotional wreck, but as I grew up as a woman, I yearned for a different life. A life of peace, joy, and purpose.

    I was looking to be a part of something that had meaning, significance, and substance. I had no idea that having a taste of something so forbidden and yet something that felt so good would bring that meaning, significance, and substance to my life. I have always struggled with having good self-esteem. I am unsure if being sexually molested as a child and later ganged-raped as a teenager is a reason for my struggle with healthy self-esteem and self-worth, but I found myself trying hard not to allow everyone to see my emotional wounds and insecurities. Some people just could no matter what I do. But even as I struggle with deep insecurities sometimes, I always make sure that my hair and eyebrows are done and I wrap myself in neat and nice clothing to compliment my body type, with a smile as a cherry on top.

It was late November of 2018 when Andre James and I officially met. He was a handsome, buff-built kind of man. When I initially set my light brown eyes on him, I thought of him as a cuddly teddy bear, warm and soft. He was a businessman, a very fine one. He spoke with class and could grab everyone's attention whenever he spoke. A lot of people gravitated toward Andre because there was something about him that knew how to stir up the nerve inside of you to dream big. His spiritual charisma was what attracted people to do business with him.

A close friend and I wanted to buy homes, and we were lucky to have met Andre because he wanted to help us. When he and I officially met, the nature of our relationship was strictly business. Within the black community, he was not only a man of spiritual providence, but he was also a salesman. He sold real estate property, and he had a special love for the black church community. He was connected to all kinds of people who were in the real estate business and who had a favor to help those within the black urban community with favorable and unfavorable credit scores. If you needed a home, no matter your credit status, Andre was divinely there to help you. He was well-known for sales negotiations such as closing costs, down payments, etc. I had a pretty good lender, and before I knew it, I was introduced to a conventional loan.

I DO, I DID, I'M **DONE!**

A conventional loan is a mortgage loan that is not insured or guaranteed by the government. Conventional loans require less paperwork and can be obtained more quickly than government-insured loans. A conventional loan was what I qualified for, and it was time to go house shopping. The goal was to look for fixer-uppers and vacant houses that were under my approved loan amount and were within the appropriate zip code that I desired.

I fell in love with house shopping. Andre and I would ride around in his car on his gas. We would go house to house prompted by our internet searches and his connections of any vacant houses within my loan price range. Andre was excited for me as a potential first-time homebuyer. He was definitely all in my process with me. It was as if he were a mentor and a guide to hold my hand throughout my process.

I genuinely felt his support and his generosity. I trusted him; we can even say we had a friendship. We shared quite a few similarities, not just being believers in Christ, but we shared some of the same trauma. We understood each other. The foundation was there, the business relationship was there, and yet there is so much more to explain.

The lines of our business relationship were crossed the very night we first met. As I previously stated, when we first met, it was strictly a business relationship for the first thirty to forty-five minutes of us first meeting each other. I was given his number by a close friend who wanted to buy a home as well, and she referred me to him since I was not able to go to the event at my church.

I called him earlier that evening and introduced myself to him. We immediately formed a bond, had a great conversation, and he told me he was out with a client and wanted to know if he could meet up with me. I remember telling him that I didn't drive, and he was happy to come to me and discuss things with me. As we conversed on the phone, he told me he was at Starbucks with a client. I exclaimed with joy because Starbucks is my favorite coffee shop. I even went on a ramble and told him the caramel Frappuccino was my favorite there. As a precaution, I had given him the address of the rental office. When he gave me a call later that evening, it was to let me know that he was parked outside.

It was dark - nighttime actually - but I walked down the street to where the rental office was located to meet him. There he stood, waiting for me like an enchanted prince, and unbelievably, in his hand was a caramel Frappuccino! This is when I realized that not only was he an active listener, but he paid attention to detail. I was smitten, not just because he bought me my favorite drink the first night we met, but because he listened to me. He cared, and he paid attention to me because he cared. Why else would he buy me something I didn't ask for on the first night of meeting him?

As we talked about the process of buying a house, his role, myself, the lender, and the seller, when I looked up, the night had gone away from us. We continued our conversation in his car because I had gotten tired of standing outside, so we eventually drove down the street and parked in front of my house. We listened to gospel music and talked about different topics.

It was then that I saw his friendly glance at me begin to turn into a more seductive look. I knew this because his stares at me became longer, he licked his lips, and his eyes were gazing at my lips. It had been a while since I had been with a man because I had spent more time with women, but I knew when someone was interested in me, no matter if it were a man or a woman.

That first night, he kissed my breast. Why did I let him? It was quite simple; I hadn't been touched by a man in quite a while. It felt good to be wanted, to be sought after, and to be ravaged. However, it was that same night that I learned he was married. Yes, he did tell me he was married. However, the night I met him, he did not have a ring on. When he gave me a hug and said goodnight, he told me he had to get home to his wife. I was perplexed because there was no ring on this man's finger, so why was he making up such a story? Was this a game for him, or was he married? I went to bed that night confused.

Over time, our business and personal relationships began to intertwine deeper. We went house shopping, and we also went to the movies and out to eat together. We graduated from flirting to official physical contact when he showed me the first house, which I thought was worth buying. He was a Pillsbury Dough Boy in public, but in private he was a lion. He was sexually aggressive at the right angle and limit. He knew how to arouse me with the right amount of control, direction, and chemistry. It was a sealed deal, and we couldn't turn the hands of time back. The bond between us began to look more surreal, and it was hard to catch the red flags in between.

While my head is in the clouds, I want to make things clear. I had never slept with a married man before Andre. This was new to me, and I was raised better and knew not to do what I was doing. I was surprised at myself. Why was I doing this? Had I lost my mind? Child, I was so perplexed about him being married because of course he did not behave like a married man, and he also didn't wear his wedding band around me.

He would mention his wife and his children here and there, but to this day, I am still unsure if he and his wife lived with each other or if they lived in separate houses. I say this because he had the availability to not only work as late as he wished because of his profession, but he also stayed until midnight sometimes with me. But what realtor do you know is showing houses late after hours?

The bondage and the sexcapades were fun until they weren't. The line was crossed when he refused to differentiate between being aggressive when we joined ourselves together and when we joined ourselves in a business relationship. His demeanor towards me had changed drastically. Before I could blink my eyes, his hand was around my neck, pushing my body up against a wall in my home. I was terrified when he did this, and things seemed to escalate quickly to other things that were much more alarming to me.

I was a single woman, but he had a lot more to lose than I did, including his family. This made his behavior more alarming in instances where his hands would move quicker than he would think. As I look back now, things could have gotten a lot worse. However, I am grateful that he and I were given a chance to walk away from one another. That was most certainly God, and no credit goes to me or Andre.

Unfortunately, I didn't get the house, but I gained peace after he and I parted ways. Yes, he was still with his wife. He never contacted me again, for which I thank God. I recall ripping up the contract where I signed over my soul to him, and it felt so good to start over, to reflect, and to spend time with God, myself, and my loved ones.

This affair showed me that in times of loneliness, God is there to spend time with him and connect with his word. God has more for me, and the best that I could do for my life, I thought, was to have fun with a married man until it wasn't fun anymore. God does not want that for me or him. He has a plan, and having patience and endurance during lonely times really develops our character so that we can stand tall and flee from tempting situations with God's help.

If you are in a sexual relationship with a married person, it may begin steamy, tempting, and exciting, but there is always a risk when being with a married person in general and especially sexually. Sometimes you can walk away from each other and never speak again, and then there are times when the consequences of our choices have to settle a debt with us.

Andre made me feel sexy, attractive, fun, and vibrant whenever I was with him. But I also had these attributes when he wasn't with me. I had fun, but then I was also afraid. I laughed, but I also cried. I released some tension, but then I kept secrets from my loved ones. I started with a dream of being a homeowner, but I ended up not getting that dream home. I started with excitement and was down for the ride, but when it was over, all I felt was joy and freedom that God had delivered me again from my crazy choices. I give God all of the praise. I forgive myself, and I forgive Andre as well. Ladies and gentlemen, a tempting ride is not worth it if it means losing your family. God has more for you.

"Don't settle for a relationship that won't let you be yourself."

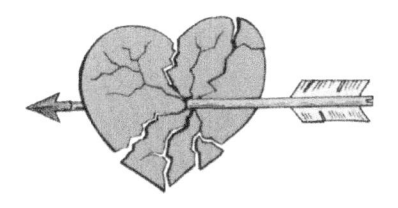

Journey 11

A Series of Unfortunate Events

Once upon a time, in a faraway kingdom nestled near the Pacific Ocean of the west coast of the United States, there lived a kind and courageous young princess who suffered in silence. From the time she was three to four years of age, she can remember that her parents, the king, and queen of South Central Los Angeles would drink so much, followed by big fights and breaking objects. She remembers the king's scar on his head, placed there by the queen (mother).

There was terror in the land, and it appeared no place was safe. After a few years of fighting, the queen (mother) separated and left the king. The young princess would long for and miss her father the king tremendously. More sadness would reign in her heart when she lost her brother at the age of five. What made matters worse, when queen (mother) grew sick, she struggled with drinking more alcohol and drugs.

Queen (mother) would parade her gentleman callers, who preyed on the young princess. She was violated by these male suitors, and she felt less than human as a result. Even in the fields of the kingdom, predators circled the kingdom. Was no place safe for a young princess?

Then, when you think life is over, you wake up. Wake up to the reality that your fairy tale nightmare was true. You were molested. You were raped. You were abandoned and unloved. Your father was missing. Your brother is dead. And you were living in the concrete jungles of Los Angeles. This was very much your reality.

This was my reality as I was dreaming of having a different life. Sad and lonely most days, I threw myself into the fantasy of books. On other days, I went outside and prayed for a kind face, another kid to talk to.

On the block, children gathered around the "friendly tree." I would find myself just sitting. I was 12 years old when he appeared. And for the first time, I felt life. Someone cared about me. Asked me about my day. Took walks with me. Said good morning and good night.

Long talks on the phone, watching the sunrise and hearing the television play the Star-Spangled Banner as television turned off for the morning. He wasn't my first crush. However, he was my first love.

Experiencing teenage love is part of the process of growing up and forming your identity and sense of self, including gender identity and sexual orientation. The renowned child development psychologist, Erik Erikson, described teenage love as a form of self-development as opposed to true love and intimacy.

Ah, teenage romance is like a thrilling rollercoaster in the amusement park of life! It's the moment to unearth your true self, exploring everything from your identity to your dreams. Teenage love is all about the epic quest of self-discovery rather than just hunting for "the one." I thought I had won the lottery of love. He was taller than me and had an athletic build. All the neighborhood girls thought he was "F-I-N-E." He was popular, too. All the guys admired his swag...He often carried his 36-inch radio around when he was not in football uniform. He was admired by the entire block. And he chose me...*me*, to be his girlfriend.

    I knew nothing about dating. In today's fast-paced world, dating has evolved into anything including traditional dinner dates to virtual meetups. The ways in which people connect and form relationships have become more diverse than ever. However, at the age of 12, dating was just sharing candy or food, or walking from place to place. And I finally had my person. He and I were a few years apart in age, so by the time he got to high school, it felt like we had spent a lifetime together.

    His mother became my mother. His brother was my brother. His pain was my pain. And when we talked about trauma and being molested, we shared experiences. He really understood me. He was going off to the military when he graduated high school. So, when he gave me the diamond promise ring, I knew he was my forever.

    I never saw heathy relationships, so I did not know what it should look like. I just knew it felt right. I loved his family, and anything was safer than going to my mother's home.

    My belief in forever was so strong. When he went out of the county for military service, I knew he was coming back. I wanted to believe his words. I would hold on to the song by The Temprees and hear the melody, "*You're a thousand miles away, But I still have your love to remember you by. Oh, my darling, dry your eyes, Daddy's coming home soon. It may be on a Sunday morning; it may be on a Tuesday afternoon. No matter what the day, I'm going to make it my business to get home soon.*"

He would call me, write letters, and even send pictures. I would write him letters, bake cookies, and accept collect calls. I was in love. "You're a thousand miles away" was my theme song and how I endured the wait. And he did return.

He returned, just after I finished testing out of high school. I tried to date another boy, and it was an epic failure. So, when he returned, I felt like Prince Charming had returned to Cinderella. I lived on Disney fairy tales, and I believed my rescue had come from the torture of my family drama. And when he drove me to get the wedding ring, I knew he was the savior of my life. I could get away from this kingdom and join him as his wife.

The romance of nurturing the relationship was everything. At eighteen, we married. By nineteen, I was pregnant. And I believed I had escaped prison to embrace the journey of marital bliss and true love.

A blind heart can help make things more painful than life. In retrospect, the unraveling of the connection should have started when the first girl showed up. She was thirteen and wanted to kick my butt.

"He is mine, and I am pregnant with his baby."

No, my naive self-did not pay attention. I married him soon after graduating high school.

By the end of the second year of marriage, child support paperwork came for children, twins.

When I questioned him, he said, "It's not mine."

I asked him if he had sex with her and he did not deny that. So, when I asked him to do the DNA test he refused.

When another girl called his cell phone and told me she was his girlfriend, I still didn't break up with him. And when he would not help with our kid, I did not break up with him. He was unemployed with no money, and I did not break up with him. When he hit me, I didn't break up with him.

We separated eventually. And I still believed his poop smelled like roses. I wanted my family. I wanted my husband, the man I loved since I was twelve years old. Could you blame me?

Then, I got that call. The call that would change my life. The call that started a series of unfortunate events. It was this call that made me rethink what love and commitment were. Everyone has boundaries, values, and principles. You have to decide where you stand and illuminate the depths of self to unveil the treasures within.

I can still hear the pain of her voice. My husband...the one I shared my life, my pain, my suffering, and invested my life in. He was a child molester.

I hit the floor. *How*? *Why*? We both were hurt as kids, so why would he hurt someone else? Nothing he said fixed it. It was at this moment, I realized that I had finally found what broke me. And, I finally had the courage and the will to say, "Boy, BYE!"

The tearing and ripping of a part of marriage is hard. Poor communication is usually the start, followed by unmet emotional needs. Often sex is the illusion that the two really care about each other.

Infidelity is hard. Domestic violence is hard. However, it was child abuse that finally broke me. And this tale, which seemed to start as one of true teen love, turned into a life lesson about being true to your principles.

I deserved better. I learned to love me. I walked away to embrace that God would lead me into that destiny which would unveil the perfect harmony in its divine time. I had to nurture my strength to move forward and soar over the peaks and valleys in the roads of life. The shame, embarrassment, and humiliation were followed by two more suicidal attempts and a parade of suicide thoughts. I tried taking my life and couldn't even get that right.

God sent several "angels" to guard my life. Counseling helped me change my views about myself, and helped me to see, that those scars could be transformed into beauty marks, too. I now look at my past and see that I survived, I lived, and I have hope! Storms gave me water, which germinated my growth. Broken wings can learn to fly again, and eagles sure do fly high! Please be encouraged to stand true to your values and love yourself first. It's ok to leave and walk away from toxic and unhealthy men and relationships, in search of true love with your yourself, first.

"If a person disregards your feelings, ignores your needs and treats you in a damaging way, distance yourself."

I DO, I DID, I'M **DONE!**

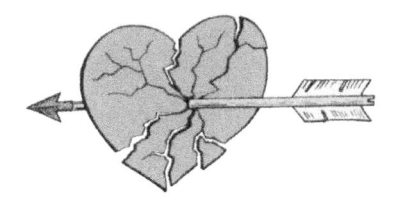

Journey 12

Blindsided

He ghosted me. Just like that. Six months after the fact. The first five and a half months were pure bliss. I thought he was my person. Then, he switched up on me.

We met online. I wasn't looking for a relationship. I just wanted a friend to hang out with from time to time. He said he was looking for a long-term relationship yet wanted to get to know me. He was willing to establish a friendship with me and continue his search for long term love.

We chatted through the dating app for about a week. I loved how clear he communicated. He was responsive, detailed, engaging, and he could spell. He was charismatic and funny, too.

Our first phone call lasted for more than an hour. We clicked immediately. There was a lot of laughing and no gaps in communication. The conversation flowed effortlessly. It was as if we had known one another all of our lives.

From then on we talked daily for sometimes up to eight hours. Yes, eight hours. We called it cupcaking and we did it all day and all night sometimes. He worked night shift, so I adjusted my schedule to his because I was self-employed.

It did not take long for me to change my mind about a relationship. Although I said I only wanted friendship, that was a cover for my heart. Deep down I desired commitment, but I was in a place on my journey where I did not believe what I desired was even possible.

The day before we connected, I prayed. In fact, I cried myself to sleep while praying. I was frustrated about a situationship I had been dealing with off and on for a while. I poured my heart out in prayer citing specific desires pertaining to a man and a committed relationship. During the first phone call with this guy, he mentioned some of the very things I had prayed about. It shocked me and scared me a bit.

The more we talked, the more he fit the bill. It was organic as he called it. My curiosity was piqued. I enjoyed being on the phone with him. He was smart, funny, engaging, and communicated so well. I was impressed. He was clear, direct, expressive, transparent, and intentional. He was aware of himself, where he was in life, where he had been, and where he was going. He also knew exactly what he wanted in a woman and partner.

I resided in California; he resided in Nevada. That wasn't a problem because initially I didn't want a relationship, right? One day, while on the phone he told me that he was coming to California. I thought he was coming to visit family and friends and might have added me to the agenda. He cleared that up and told me that he was coming to see me and might add them to the agenda if time permits. I was flattered. Too easily.

I thought he was attractive in his photos. He was dark skinned, with a bald head, and had an amazing smile. I made jokes about his height. If he was short, I told him that it wasn't going to work even being my friend. I was excited to meet him in person.

A week later, he showed up in the middle of the day (as planned). He offered to take me to a late lunch and when I asked where we should go, he suggested Mexican food and stated he knew it was my favorite. He remembered. I was flattered, again. Too easily.

We went to one of my favorite restaurants, had lunch, drinks, and laughed.

From across the table at the restaurant, he looked at me and stated, "You know you're off the market, right?"

I giggled.

"I really don't see anything funny," he sarcastically replied.

Then, he got up from his seat, walked around to my seat and came close. The way he looked at me and leaned in I thought something was wrong with my face.

He gently lifted my chin, leaned down, and kissed me. Once, twice, and three times. My body was flooded with warmth and nervousness. I was not a kisser at all. I mean, I did not like to kiss, and I just wasn't an affectionate person. In the moment, I did not know if I was offended about the kisses... or if I liked them.

I sipped my drink while blushing and the more I gave it thought I realized I liked the kisses. I could still feel his lips on mine, and I wanted more but there was no way I was going to tell him that.

By the time we met in person, I already determined that I liked this guy. Clearly, he liked me too. He spent his off day driving from Las Vegas, Nevada to Redlands, California, to meet me. The night before he arrived, we video chatted for the first time. It was cute because as much as we talked by telephone, when the cameras were on, all we could do was smile and laugh.

After lunch/dinner, we headed to Newport Beach. The drive down was filled with music we had shared with one another over the prior two weeks. We shared a brief conversation and the time together just felt good. He held my hand while driving and when he needed both hands to navigate the vehicle, my hand rested on his leg. We were comfortable with one another.

We walked the beach without shoes, hand in hand. There was a beautiful sunset that evening. We took pictures and just enjoyed one another. It was sweet and romantic. Everything about being with him felt right.

At one point, he walked up and embraced me. It felt good in his arms. He stood 6'4', athletic build, strong, yet gentle. So, when he wrapped his arms my 5'7" plus sized body, it was a treat. I especially enjoyed standing on my tippy toes to kiss him and looking up to him to look into his eyes.

By the time the sunset, I had kissed him several more times. He told me at the restaurant that I was going to crave his kisses one day and he was right. I craved his kisses, his hugs, his touch, and him the rest of that day and for the duration of our relationship.

The next few months were filled with me traveling to Vegas to see him and him traveling to Redlands to see me. We saw one another weekly, or at least every other week. We spent the night together more than seven times before we became intimate. I was amazed at his level of self-control and discipline. He told me early on that he didn't want to lead with sex and that sex was not that important to him. He was on a mission to find his person, the woman for him, and desired to cultivate a relationship like the one his parents had.

Honestly, I thought he had issue with his male part because he exhibited so much self-control. I knew he was attracted to me and for the life of me I couldn't understand how he could spoon me to sleep and not try anything. I was ready much earlier than I should have been, but he led that entire process, and I am glad he did it the way he did. To me, that said a lot about him, and it made me like him more.

His parents have been married for more than 54 years. They are a beautiful couple. I watched them love on one another, holding hands, rubbing feet, serving each other in love. I was careful to observe them when he took me to Washington state to meet them the week before and of Christmas. I wanted to know exactly what it was that he admired about their union to determine if I could do my part in creating something similar with him to what they had.

We went from becoming acquainted, to officially dating, to exclusively dating, to a committed relationship. He was clear and intentional about what he wanted. He was sure about himself, and he was sure about me. I liked that. No, I loved it! He led the relationship from one phase to the next and I willingly followed his lead because I liked how he moved.

He was open and honest, gave me access to his

home, leaving me there while he worked at times. In fact, on most of my visits, I would arrive at his condo by myself, let myself in, while he was at work. I'd cook for him, to ensure he had a hot meal when he got off from work. I'd tidy the place and await his arrival. He gave me an open door to come over, to call, to leave items at his place so that I could easily drive up to see him at the drop of a dime with no worry.

He did not seem like the type who would play games, lie and be deceitful. He was a complete gentleman, opening doors, pulling out chairs, covering the tab, sending sweet text messages with emojis, calling every day, cooking for me...I mean, he was on it. He held me as I fell asleep several times without crossing the line. I did not know how much I needed those moments.

He was very affectionate and while I was not typically affectionate in relationships, I liked this guy so much and I liked how he handled me, so I rolled with the affection. I started to like it a lot. We would cuddle on his couch and watch tv. If I didn't fall asleep in his arms or on his chest, he fell asleep in my arms or on my chest.

We kissed a lot. He taught me to kiss without knowing he was teaching me. He was gentle, patient, and made it easy for me to relax in his company.

We took pictures together. I have about 1,000 photos in my phone right now from the six-month journey because every time we were together, I took pictures. He was with it, and I loved that.

For Christmas I got us matching pajamas. He wore them and took pictures with me in them. He told me he'd do anything to make me happy. He told me that I was his purpose and his priority. I believed him based on his actions and how he treated me.

Taking me to meet his parents, his family, and friends was the icing on the cake. My family and close friends were excited for us because meeting the parents usually means something really good. I mean, he even told me before our trip that he was ready to commit to me because he didn't want to take me home as someone he was just dating. I had to be his woman, his girlfriend. I was honored to be.

By the start of month four, I had grown to love him. One day I mustered the courage to tell him. By then, he had already presented the idea of us moving in together, we had talked about marriage, and we had become active in business together.

He showed up for me, I showed up for him. We talked about any and everything. We even discussed the hard things that could come up with aging parents, health, unstable adult children, and so much more. This was the easiest most natural flowing relationship I had ever had. I did not think we would face anything that we could not overcome.

I wasn't trying to impress him when we met. I laid my truth on the table and either he liked me, or he didn't and if he didn't so what! It turned out that he liked me, and I thought that was a treat.

The way things ended was abrupt and painful! This guy went from the most attentive, endearing, affectionate man with stellar communication to a mean, cold hearted, distant stranger. It was during month five that I noticed he wasn't as responsive to my text messages. I thought the relationship was changing for the better, so this was no big deal, plus we talked on the phone daily for hours at a time.

Then, I noticed that he stopped sending text messages and he wasn't reading my love notes and responding to them like he had been doing all along. No big deal, right?! Yet, I noticed the change.

For New Year's Eve, I had planned to make him gumbo and be at his house waiting for him when he got off from work. When I mentioned my plans to visit him, he told me that he had plans with some of his guy friends from out of town. That was the first time he declined me coming to visit him. I didn't think much of it. My feelings were a little hurt, but his friends were in town, and I understood. Besides, we had just returned from Washington, spent the week leading to Christmas together, and I still went to his house the weekend after New Year's.

When I got there, the items he told me to leave were all in place, my perfume and personal items were on the bathroom sink, the card I gave him was on the refrigerator, my clothes were where I left them, and my snacks still in the kitchen. All signs of a bachelor's pad with a hint of "he's got a woman" were all over his condo. That warmed my heart.

When I did see him later that week, we had a great time but for the next visit he came to see me. His ex called while we were together and there was a weird energy between us after that. I learned during that visit that she was still driving one of his trucks.

This man was solid, and he was an upstanding man as far as I could tell. He told me if I relocated to Vegas with my son and things didn't work out between us that he was committed to making sure me and my son were good no matter what. He even suggested that we maintain living together until my son, who was a sophomore, graduated high school in order to provide a stable home for him, in the event our relationship failed for some reason. I knew if he'd make that sort of commitment to me, then he offered something similar to the ex, hence the reason she still had one of his cars.

I tried to be supportive and understanding. I also trusted him and whatever deal they made before me was just that – before me. I did not like the fact that he did not disclose those details prior to us entering a committed relationship, however I was ten toes down by this point, so I was willing to ride it out.

During the following visit, we bumped heads for the first time. It was simply a miscommunication. I failed to bring to his attention a broken taillight on a car we were delivering for the business we now shared. He flipped. He was angry! In fact, he was so angry, I assumed something else had triggered his emotional response.

When I asked what was wrong, he said, "I just don't understand why you didn't say anything!"

I was shocked to learn he was angry with me. Especially over the matter at hand. My feelings were hurt, and I was emotional, but I fought the release of tears. My cycle was due, so my hormones were wacky, plus I had found seven strands of hair in his bed the night before. Yep.

Listen, I am a black woman and I wear weaves, but that was Becky's hair, do you hear me? I calmly brought it to his attention that night after he got home from work and was settled. I didn't flip out, but I was triggered. Believe me, I was triggered.

He downplayed it. He told me the comforter on the bed had been in the closet for a while and maybe that's where the hair came from. I knew he had been in a committed relationship with "Becky" before me, so I accepted his explanation. From that day on, however, I was on guard.

My feelings were hurt about his blowing up over the taillight and I was still recovering over finding the hair, so I expressed that, we talked, we hugged, kissed and all was well. Three weeks later, he stopped me mid-sentence while on the phone and told me that he was tired of me bringing up my ex in every conversation we had. I was shocked. I didn't know what he was talking about. As a communicator, I am intentional and calculated with my words. I was quite sure that I had not been bringing my ex up in "every" conversation like he accused me of.

When I told him this, his response was, "So are you saying I'm a liar."

I didn't want to say he was a liar because I didn't want to argue. I just made a mental note to never mention an ex or any man when we talked again.

Two weeks after that, we got into it over social media. I posted a photo of our date and his ex, supposedly the one who still drove his truck, messaged him about it. Never mind the fact that his ex was stalking my page, and the picture did not include his face or my face or any part of our bodies. There was nothing in the picture that even suggested we were together, but she was watching and adding things up. But why was she watching my page and why did her thoughts or feelings matter enough for him to bring it to my attention?

We got into so bad over that, I almost broke up with him. In fact, I did break up with him. I told him I was done. He could have Becky and he could kiss my social media ass basically. He was determined to resolve the matter. He made every effort for us to talk it through and he dismissed my emotional response of alluding to breaking up. He completely dismissed it, so that meant we were still together. For me, I was slowly detaching and backing away because I did not like the turn of events and fear was starting to surface.

The following week, I posted a photo of our faces on social media and apparently that rubbed the ex the wrong way, too. When he came at me about that, it escalated to the point of an argument. I was done and ready to walk away because things were not adding up.

This man spent countless hours on the phone deliberating and trying to get me to understand his point of view after I said I was done. He pleaded with me, and I was so frustrated that I prayed right then and there on the phone call. After I prayed, I was able to hear and understand him better. It was enough for me to give things another shot because what we had been cultivating was worth so much more than a spat over social media triggered by an ex who was irrelevant. So, I thought.

He came to visit me the following week and we had a beautiful time. He stayed a couple of days. We went to dinner, went to the movies, had Chinese take-out, cuddled, and watched movies. We made love, to me, for the first time. Our hunger for one another was obvious before he even arrived. From the moment we saw each other we embraced like it had been forever. The way he kissed me this time was different. He looked deeply into my eyes while making love and I felt something in my soul. I thought we were good and smooth sailing again.

While managing one of our business projects, two photos popped up. One included a woman on his doorstep.

When I inquired about it, he went stupid, as in he didn't know who she was. Only to turn around and tell me who she was. He said it was a friend. But there was more to it. Let's just say he didn't like being questioned, he didn't like me pointing out his lack, he didn't like being told anything about himself.

I told him I didn't like what I saw, what I was hearing, or how I felt. I am not an insecure woman and yet there I was feeling insecure. I did not understand how he was so open and transparent from the beginning and all along to now women popping up by the house, his truck that Becky was driving in the driveway, just all kinds of things that were not adding up.

I was super sensitive, feeling insecure, and needed reassurance and validation that he failed to provide. I was on edge about everything at this point. We were on the phone while he was at work, and he needed to call me back. Two hours passed and he hadn't called yet, which was unlike him. I called him. He didn't answer nor call me back. I texted him an hour later to tell him I was going to bed. It was after 1 am.

I fell asleep and woke up around 2:15 am expecting to see a response to my text. Nothing. By now, he was off from work but why hadn't he called me or texted me? This was not his usual pattern. I knew something was off. Intuition is real and we must learn to trust it!

I texted him calling him out for being inconsistent and having divided attention lately. I asked him what was going on. My initial suspicion was not another women. Although that did cross my mind. I was always careful to give him the benefit of the doubt.

He called me back immediately, but not to talk, to

argue. We had an argument over me asking why he didn't reply to my text or call me back. He always calls me from work. For six months straight. And he almost always answered my calls, returned my calls right away if he so happened to miss it, and responded to my text messages quickly and lovingly... until recently and in that moment.

He tried to use the excuse that he was at work. He even argued that sometimes he won't be able to call me or text me when he's at work. Listen, I am a businesswoman with strong work ethics. I get that but this was not the usual for us, okay?! His job was easy, and the night shift was dead most of the time. The big wigs were gone by the time he started his shift. He could get away with murder at his job and I knew it. We had a routine of talking for hours while he was at work. Even when he was with customers he'd have me on the phone, and I'd listen to his interactions with them. Even when he was engaged in conversations with his coworkers he'd have me on the phone. Lunch breaks, bathroom runs, all of it – I was on the phone regularly. So why was he trying to make excuses all of a sudden?

The call ended but on a calm note and with him stating he would call me later. We were both upset but it was such a petty matter that I knew we'd get passed it. I needed reassurance and validation based on his behavior change and the recent discoveries. He was dismissive and evasive instead. I was hurt but I knew we'd talk more about it another time.

Well, we didn't. He didn't call me later that day like he said. Three days later and still no call, no text. I called once on day two and there was no answer. He was visible on social media, so he wasn't dead. He also picked up one of the cars from the transportation business, based on the app notes, so he wasn't disabled. For some reason, he just wasn't talking to me or reaching out to me... suddenly. Something was up. Big time.

To me, if you *no show no call*, you're fired. We weren't dating, we were in a relationship. This was not how you treat your partner. I was hurt but even more so I was confused.

On day four, I had to text him about the business. He responded to my text but made no mention of anything else. It was the weirdest and most painful thing. We ended up having to engage in a phone call about the business because a client could not find the vehicle and I attempted to talk to him about us. He was evasive, dismissive, and very strategic about what he would say. My intuition told me he was in the presence of a woman. In fact, after a little research, I saw her in another photo through our business account. Men can be so stupid and sloppy. That was all the confirmation I needed.

I don't know what changed and when. I don't know why things were so good until they weren't. I don't know why this man introduced me to his parents, and his close friends. I don't know why he spent Valentine's Day, which was his birthday, with me. I don't know why we had a beautiful visit a week prior to him ghosting me, with passionate love making at play. I don't know why he told me I was his purpose and his priority or why he initiated talks about marriage, moving in together, etc. But I do know that I prayed and asked God to reveal and expose what I needed to know. Granted, we were fornicating but that didn't stop me from praying. I learned a long time ago that we can't let sin cause us to run from God. That's when we need him the most anyway.

I didn't go searching for evidence of infidelity. I didn't intentionally look to sabotage what seemed like the easiest relationship I have ever had. I was happy with my man and proud to be his woman. I was completely smitten! There is a hint of me in every room of his condo. I made sure of it simply by adding what I identified as needed. That's just how I roll. From the vitamins in his medicine cabinet, to the dish towels in the linen closet, to custom coffee mugs in the kitchen and so much more. He'll think of me for sure and he'll miss me now that I am gone.

I added value to his life in so many ways and he admitted that which is why I can't understand how we got here. I prayed for him and over him. When he would get out of the shower I would massage his body and lotion him down and pray while doing so. Anytime I was at his house, I would make sure a hot meal was waiting for him when he got in from work. I made the bed, I washed dishes, did laundry, vacuumed the floor, and we didn't live together. I bought candles and aromatherapy products for his place. I managed the communication for his business, helped him with his child support issues, helped him with banking and finances, ordered gifts for his grandchildren (he paid, I shopped) and I supported every idea he had by taking action. Again, he acknowledged my efforts and thanked me for them. Anytime I asked if there were any issues that needed to be addressed, he never had a complaint. He told me over and over that I was a good woman. Perhaps I was too good....for him.

I tried to talk to my man about the changes I noticed in his behavior, and he shut me out for the first time. Then, he did the very thing I had a problem with by not calling or reaching out at all... As if he was punishing me or making a point. I'm too old to play those games and so is he (He's in his 50's).

I made it easy for both of us and ended things. What more was there to discuss at this point? What could he say to redeem himself? I wrote him a letter. Well, I typed it. This wasn't unusual as I sent him love notes and love letters all the time. I used to leave them in random places in his condo, so he'd find them when I wasn't there, and he'd be reminded of how much he meant to me. This new letter was my departure notice. It was my closure. I was going to bow down gracefully and just walk away, however expressing my feelings in writing has always been therapeutic. After a friend recommended that I get it out, I did, and I felt much better. I don't know if he read it or if he will ever read it. It wasn't for him. It was for me.

We went from having the most amazing relationship and connection, with easy, stellar communication, open conversations, talking every day for hours, and talking about anything, to not even being able to discuss breaking up if that's what we were doing. Even his mother showed more care and concern about my broken heart.

She and I spoke weekly and that's the main reason I informed her of where things stood. I knew I would need some time away from our calls. I don't believe you have to cut off family members you genuinely connect with while in a relationship with someone once the relationship ends. It's really a case-by-case ordeal. I'll venture to say that I am most likely not the first heart he has broken, and his mother is well aware. Usually, we know our children and their patterns.

After he refused to talk to me because he was laid up with someone else and thought I didn't know, I blocked him. I removed myself from the business, after being responsible and taking care of a few key things, including two clients I had been working with. I wrote him that letter, emailed it, and I purposed in my heart and mind to move on. Just like that.

    I loved him. I still do. But sometimes you can love someone with every fiber of your being and still have to let them go. I said I was done with toxic men and relationships a few years ago. I said I was done with old patterns of unhealthy situations. This became unhealthy. It was no longer safe for me emotionally and that's a huge problem. We have to be brave enough to draw the line and not cross it, even if an apology is extended. Some things should just not occur when you value and respect the other person. His actions and inaction showed me that he did not value or respect me. He may have liked me but that was not enough.

"The moment that you start to wonder if you deserve better, you do."

ABOUT THE LEAD AUTHOR & ANTHOLOGIST

Tanya Denise is the Founder & Executive Director of the International Association of Women Authors (IAWA), the world's leading global network for women who write. She is a self-published, international, best-selling author, anthologist, book and writing coach. Born Latanya Hampton, in Pasadena, California, Tanya has been writing since she was a young girl, beginning her journey with poetry and short stories, then gradually growing into newsletters, newspapers, independent magazines, journals, then books.

Tanya is a serial entrepreneur, and she is a certified Domestic Violence Specialist. Her first anthology series titled, *Pretty Sad* includes five volumes of stories about the extraordinary strength of women who have overcome trauma, including abuse, addiction, depression, prostitution, and more. *Pretty Sad* is the first book series under the #timetotell movement. The movement was created by Tanya to help women tell their stories of going from tragedy to triumph! *Pretty Sad* was the #1 new release on Amazon in December 2019 and became a best seller!

In 2018, Tanya founded Love Wins Publishing (www.lovewinspub.com), to assist new and aspiring female writers in becoming published authors. She has published more than 55 of her own books, including journals, anthologies, workbooks, self-help books, devotionals, and her memoir. In addition, Tanya has helped more than 400 writers become first-time published authors.

In 2023, Tanya founded Writer's Block Press (WBP), (www.writersblockpress.com) and now oversees multiple publishing companies. WPB is an emerging publishing house that aims to revolutionize the world of literature and bring forth a new era of literary excellence. The company serves women, men, and children writers.

Tanya has a heart for helping others. Her passion has led to the receipt of several community awards, including Woman of the Year by the Antelope Valley Ad Hoc Committee on Education. Tanya's purpose is to utilize her proven faith in God to serve as a catalyst to help others heal and operate in their gift(s). Her mission is to use her gift of writing to help women and empower them to walk in their purpose.

With a passion for finance, Tanya is a licensed insurance agent, and she enjoys traveling, spending time with her loved ones, and trying new restaurants. Tanya is an enthusiastic writer, speaker, and book coach. She currently resides in Southern California.

For speaking engagements and or more information, please visit www.authortanyadenise.com

Made in the USA
Middletown, DE
31 August 2024